Get More P...
...Your Employees will Love You for it!

How to turn your existing recognition and incentive expenses into profits

By John Schaefer
America's Employee Recognition Expert

and creator of

The Vocational Shrink Communications Training Program

Illustrations by Brian Freeman

Forward by Warren Struhl
Owner and Chief Inspiration Officer at Successories, Inc.

Art Direction and Design by
Patty H. Findley
Turn Key Design, Tucson, Arizona

All rights reserved. Everything in this book is protected by copyright law. Reproduction by any means, electronic or mechanical, including photocopying, recording or by any information retrieval system without written permission from the author, except for the inclusion of brief quotations in a review, is strictly prohibited.

Copyright 2010 by John Schaefer
America's Employee Recognition Expert

To all of my clients, colleagues, friends and associates who travel *The Ten Levels* with me as we all strive for recognition, fulfillment and growth in our work while seeking a more rewarding and happy life.

John Schaefer
America's Employee Recognition Expert

Schaefer Recognition Group
7131 W. Planada Lane · Glendale, AZ 85310
(888) 646-6670
www.SchaeferRecognitionGroup.com
john@SchaeferRecognitionGroup.com

Acknowledgments

This work is the culmination of a series of events, awareness's and personal experiences along with the creative input of my co-workers. Mixed with a lifelong appreciation of both the frailty and tenacity of human beings, I have been able to capture some of the good and bad, obvious and subtle, serious and funny, and ultimately, the successful and flawed ways that people survive in the American workplace.

My curiosity, research, failures and successes have led me to develop solutions for the What, Why and How of the American workplace:

What are your employees doing?
Why are they doing it?
How can you fix it?

I am forever grateful to and appreciative of:

- My wife Sandy, son Ian, and daughters Rachael and Sarah for consistently being examples of the best characteristics of human beings, and for believing in me as I have pondered what work, family and life are all about.

- Larry, for the time and the deep belly laughs we had as *The Ten Levels* took shape, so many years ago.

- Doug, for his friendship and help in developing my spiritual insights that gave this book a happy ending and let my life take on a whole new level of meaning.

- All of the co-workers, colleagues, managers, artists, designers, factories and suppliers from whose struggles, victories, frustrations, and decisions I was able to make this book both fun to read and meaningful to study.

Get More Productivity for Less Money . . . Your Employees will Love You for It

Table of Contents

Acknowledgments — iii

Foreword — ix

Introduction – Three Strikes and You're IN! — xi
How My Love of Baseball can Help you Improve Workplace Morale, Productivity and Profit.

Part I – What are Your Employees Doing? — 1

An Analysis of the *Ten Levels of Workplace Disillusionment*.

Chapter 1 – *The Ten Levels of Workplace Disillusionment* — 7

- **Level 1** – Your New Employees are in a State of **Disbelief**
- **Level 2** – Soon, They May Resort to **Nodding and Agreeing**
- **Level 3** – Your Problems Begins with **Griping and Complaining**
- **Level 4** – If You're Not Careful, You May Lose them to **Escape** Habits
- **Level 5** – **Gut Check**, One Last Chance to Win them Back
- **Level 6** – Beware the **Class Clown** . . . He Can Cost You Money!
- **Level 7** – True **Apathy**; The Point of No Return for Many
- **Level 8** – The Sadness and Waste of **Decline and Surrender**
- **Level 9** – Some of your Scarier Employees may Develop **Paranoia**
- **Level 10** – **Insanity**, Beyond Help, But Fortunately There are Few

Chapter 2 – Some Common Trends　　　　　73

- Cyclic Trends –These Symptoms Just Keep Coming Back!
- Self-Maintaining Trends – You Can Lose Some Here!
- Hints to Identifying Levels – Quick Guide to Idiosyncrasies

Chapter 3 – Make Changes in Your　　　　　87
　　　　　　Workplace and Your Life

- How to Get Off the Merry-go-Round
- A Ray of Sunlight in the Storm

Part II – Why are They Doing It?　　　　　97

What the experts say about emotional engagement and the secret to turning recognition expenses into profits.

Chapter 4 – What Went Wrong　　　　　99
　　　　　　With Traditional Recognition Programs
The Top Five Recognition Objections.

Chapter 5 – The Five Biggest Mistakes　　　　　103
　　　　　　Managers Make in Recognizing their Employees
They're costing you money, but are easy to fix.

Chapter 6 – Cash Just Isn't Enough!　　　　　107
How to get more from, without paying more to, employees . . . *and they'll love you for it!*

Chapter 7 – How to Turn　　　　　111
　　　　　　HR Expenses into Profits
No – body's got new money to spend, but there are some simple ways to get more returns for fewer dollars and be able to *prove it to your CFO!*

Part III – How Can You Fix It?   119

Introducing the Umbrella Recognition Solution. A strategy to save you money and improve your results while engaging both employees and their managers.

Chapter 8 – The Umbrella Recognition Solution   121
Minimizing Program Costs
- Supervisor and Employee Training
- Reinforcement/Rewards
- Measurement/Analysis
- Performance Management

Chapter 9 – The Three Steps to Successful   129
Recognition and Performance Improvement Structure and Implementation

Chapter 10 – A Combination of New and Traditional Tools   133

About the Author   139

About the Illustrator   141

Get More Productivity for Less Money . . . Your Employees will Love You for It

Foreword

For more than 25 years, we at Successories have celebrated inspiration and motivation. We've always believed in the power of a sincere and timely pat on the back to show people how much they are truly valued and respected.

When I met John Schaefer I was immediately impressed with how much his beliefs mirrored mine, yet he comes at recognition from a different perspective. As an employee recognition expert with 25 years of experience, John sees the same values and benefits as I do, but he focuses on educating an organization's management team about the proper use of recognition. He and his team teach the importance of genuine and meaningful communications in developing effective recognition and incentive programs for his clients.

The synergy of ideas we share is skillfully presented in this powerful book. Our mutual goal is to help organizations understand how they will benefits from a comprehensive communications strategy that combines all aspects of awards, rewards, recognition and performance improvement. The combined resources of our two firms allows us to present a simple, viable and timely solution to a human resources challenge that has traditionally been fragmented and hard to quantify.

Beginning with his entertaining, yet poignant, *Ten Levels of Workplace Disillusionment,* John leads us though the What, Why and How of corporate recognition. His wit and easy language lead you on an intriguing journey through the problems, solutions and practical tools that many companies are looking for to optimize their investments in employees.

In *"Get More Productivity for Less Money . . . Your Employees will Love You for It!"* John discusses the changes occurring in recognition as the workforce expands to include four distinct generations. You'll learn how companies are responding and receive some tips to quickly educate your managers and get them excited about using effective tools enthusiastically.

The Gallup Organization's Curt Coffman says, "The only thing worse than no recognition is insincere recognition." John Schaefer shows you how to make sure that the recognition your people receive is always the sincere kind. When you do it right, they really will love you for it!

Warren Struhl
Owner and Chief Inspiration Officer
Successories, Inc.

Introduction

Three Strikes and You're IN!

How My Love of Baseball can Help you Improve Workplace Morale, Productivity and Profit.

I've always loved baseball, but I never realized that it would come to define my style and passion for helping companies optimize their most important asset – people! Let me give you an example or what I mean. When I began speaking to groups, I quickly realized that when I was in the audience and the speaker began sharing the 10 steps, or the 12 secrets, or the 25 tips to something or other, by the time they got to step 5 or 6, I'd forget what they were steps of! So, I decided to deal with everything in threes. Like a good at-bat, it feels comfortable and keeps things simple.

Baseball is a simple game; not easy, but simple. It all began for me when I was nine years old. As the smallest guy on the team, they gave me uniform number 1 (the shirts were sized from smallest to largest back then). I was little, but spunky, fast and absorbed the game like a sponge! They put me in center field where I soon earned the nickname "The Vacuum" because I sucked up everything that went past the infield. One game, I surprised my team, the coach and all of the parents in the stands by catching a fly ball on the right centerfield wall and proceeding to throw a one-hopper to third to catch the kid on second tagging up. Not only was it a great play, but the coach didn't expect a nine year old even to understand that aspect of the game. This was the beginning of a love affair that would last a lifetime.

Get More Productivity for Less Money . . . Your Employees will Love You for It

By the time I was 12; I was the biggest guy on the team and got to wear number 15. That year I pitched and in one game struck out 17 batters. The last out was a dribbler back to the mound, so I made that play too. We lost the game (I guess I walked a few), but still got the game ball.

In 7th grade we had a guy at school that had us all bowing at his feet. Curt was bigger than everybody else, hit the ball so far that we didn't even go look for it, was dating a 10th grade cheerleader and scrimmaged with the high school basketball team on the weekends. He even had facial hair; not stubble, but the real thing! I'll never forget the day when the call came in . . . I'd been called up to play on the White Sox; Curt's team, and his dad was the coach. I got a base hit the first time up and will forever cherish the high five from Curt when I came in to score.

Well, just when you guys are beginning to whisper about who is lucky enough to have my rookie card, things took a hiatus for about 20 years. All of a sudden, everybody else grew up, I lost my nerve, went to work, began raising a family and baseball became something I just watched on TV. Like every fan, I always hoped to go to a game and catch a foul ball the dreams of the fan, not the player.

But, the story's not over yet. When my kids were young, we went to the school carnival. There we saw a big dunk tank right next to ticket booth. For $5 you got three balls and if you hit the bull's eye, the principal took a bath. "Go for it Dad, you can get 'em" (they'd heard the stories of my youth). On the second throw, whoosh, I nailed it and down went Mr. McKinney; hero again!

I thought about this feat for a couple of weeks, and sure enough, as luck would have it, I ran into a guy who was playing men's-over-30 baseball; real baseball, with metal cleats, wood bats and 90 foot base lines. "Heck yeah, I can still do this, I thought, so I told them I was a pitcher. I got my chance and after balking twice did get to strike out a couple of guys with the high hard one, but my elbow and hamstrings just weren't holding up well. Most of these guys had played college ball, some even had some minor league professional experience. They never did find out that I hadn't pitched since I was in little league, but hey, I got to run, hit, throw, smell the grass and the leather; I was a ballplayer again!

This too was short lived, as my 40-year-old body couldn't do it week after week, but let's fast forward to this year (finally!). Still the baseball freak, I go to opening day at Chase Field to watch the Arizona Diamondbacks every year. This year, my buddy (who always gets me tickets for my birthday) found us front row seats half way down the first base line in shallow right. Yep, I brought my glove!

We did the whole deal; hot dogs, beer and peanuts and watched the D-backs take the lead over the Rockies. In the seventh inning we got a text from two friends and found out that they were in our same section, about 20 rows up. We stood and waved, so they could see the cool seats we had. It was the perfect day for baseball on a warm April day. Everybody around us was into the game (hey, we were down there with the real opening day fans). Top of the ninth, first pitch and Ryan Spilborghs slices one down the right field line and it's tailing foul, coming towards our section. We're all on our feet, a couple of us braver souls stretch out over the wall as this screaming liner hooks our way. I, of course reached the farthest. Smack, ball against leather. It seemed like an eternity... somebody had caught it. I thought I felt something, so pulled up my mitt and holy cow; there was a ball in it. I was stunned, then ecstatic. I jumped up, pulled the ball out of my glove and turned to show it to my friends up above. 3,000 people went nuts and jumped to their feet. Imagine that feeling! I'd seen this happen on TV, but I never thought it would be me!

Wait, there's more!

They played it back on the jumbotron and the analyst Mark Grace voiced his approval – "That's why you bring your glove to the ball game. Nice glove work by the veteran!" I was in heaven! Here, check it out on YouTube – http://www.youtube.com/watch?v=wXi1uTxMt84.

Okay, you're all wondering; what's this got to do with recognizing employees and getting high performance in the workplace?

Glad you asked.

There are five lessons here:

1. Training – Be prepared to make the play. I spent my whole life learning the skills to make this catch. Not only that, I was ready with my glove on, still paying attention in the ninth inning and had the instinctive ability to make the play of this level without thinking. A well trained, focused, present and capable workforce not only makes more plays, but has fewer accidents, wastes less material, breaks fewer pieces of equipment, demonstrates more cooperation, achieves better productivity and makes your firm a lot more money.

2. Practice – Looking back, I realized how many hours I'd practiced the skills that ultimately made my reactionary catch possible. It was a backhand play on a fast moving baseball. Only well practiced employees are ready to instinctively do the right thing under pressure. Those few milliseconds of indecision that separate the well intentioned rookie from the well honed expert can make all the difference between a catch and a costly incident. Lost time accidents, injuries and equipment damage due to inexperienced employees continue to be one of the most expensive and wasteful areas for many companies.

3. Attitude – Have the confidence to go for it while others pull back or duck. Anybody can bare hand a little pop foul, but to snag a tailing liner you've got to have a combination of experience, confidence and guts. Employees who feel valued and respected are more likely to put in the hours and the effort to be really good at what they do; not because they fear being fired if they don't, but because they like you, appreciate the company and want be a part of a winning team. They're also a lot less likely to take their skills to your competitors when things get tough.

4. Recognition – When I turned to the stands and held up the ball, just imagine how it felt when thousands of cheering fans came to their feet in approval. It was overwhelming! Giving immediate, appropriate and genuine recognition when an employee takes a chance and it pays off is one of the most valuable things a supervisor can ever do. When your management team is ready, aware and has the proper tools at hand, this is not only easy, but soon becomes a habit that transcends the entire organization. Most people underestimate the value of an honest, timely pat on the back when it's deserved. If your team is a well-oiled machine, your supervisors will have more time to concentrate on opportunities to use recognition, because so much less time is being wasted on recruiting, training, and coaching of new employees due to higher than necessary turnover.

5. Share the Glory – When I made the play, everybody around me seemed to enjoy sharing in the moment almost as much as I did as the high-fives ensued. Let's face it, there's only so much time in the work day for celebrating success and handing out recognition. The best managers realize this, so they make sure that as many peers as possible get to participate in each recognition moment. When other team members see how often it happens, they share the love and look forward to their turn. Using both individual and team-based recognition is a great way to foster camaraderie and keep everyone more focused on the job at hand.

Now I know what you were saying. This was a lucky break, because I was in the right place at the right time. But what if we could create an environment in your workplace where this happened regularly; on purpose? That's what I'm going to share with you in this book, and here's the best news of all:

> It's fun, it's easier than you think, and
> it won't cost you any money.
> As a matter of fact, it'll make you money,
> and you'll be able to prove it to the CFO!

*"If you have a job without aggravations,
you don't have a job."*

—Malcolm Forbes

*"What do we live for if not to make the
world less difficult for each other?"*

—George Eliot, novelist

Part 1
What are Your Employees Doing?

An Analysis of *The Ten Levels of Workplace Disillusionment*

Anyone who's ever had a job has probably wondered, "Why do people (including me) react the way they do at work?"

We all expect some frustrations and stresses at work. With more options out there than ever before, how do we keep focused, rather than constantly seeing the grass as greener on the other side? Managers, how can you be sure that your best workers are fulfilled and aren't looking around at other opportunities? Recognizing some key signs of defensive behavior is part of the answer to both of these questions.

Malcolm Forbes said, "If you have a job without aggravations, you don't have a job." It's when these annoyances cause us to take on reactive, often strange, survival mannerisms that it becomes worthy of concern.

This part of the book, *The Ten Levels of Workplace Disillusionment*, will help you bring your subconscious, negative habit patterns into your conscious mind, where you can consider options for change. The ideas presented here will help allow supervisors to quickly identify the behavior patterns taken on by their employees as they struggle with various forms of company politics and office challenges. You will find here a framework to both address and help change counterproductive habit patterns in an amusing, yet compelling way. Over time, this realization and alteration of behaviors will create a workplace environment where employees can flourish and reach their peak levels of performance, while assuring your company's strong base of quality personnel, improved profitability and sustained growth.

What started out as nothing more than a couple of employees making silly assessments of fellow workers' reactions to stress in the workplace, has over 20 years turned into much more. Along the way, it has morphed into numerous forms. When we began to realize that our observations of employee behavior had certain consistencies and patterns, we slowly assembled them into the original *Ten Levels of Workplace Disillusionment* that you'll find here. At this point, these were nothing more than simple descriptions of unique employee behaviors and characteristics that we found interesting and funny.

This material was originally written as a self-help text designed to assist employees in realizing and coming to grips with their negative, reactionary habit patterns. That led to a more complete evaluation of the *Ten Levels* using fictional characters, each based on groups of real people I had worked with early in my career. I also added the chapter on Common Trends to explain some of the reoccurring paths taken through the *Ten Levels* during a career. After sharing the manuscript with friends and family, I expanded it to include some advice on how to break free from the grip of the *Ten Levels*, as well as some of my personal journey to freedom. By then, my concept for this book was fully underway.

As my growing employee recognition and incentive business, Schaefer Recognition Group (www.Schaefer-RecognitionGroup.com), grew and my territory representing The Tharpe Company (today TharpeRobbins, www.TharpeRobbins.com) provided me with a wide range of experiences helping organizations recognize and motivate their employees, the idea of *The Vocational Shrink – The Game* began to take shape. Employer/employee communication needs improvement and offering a tool that can be played as a game really sounded like a great concept to me.

Having realized that so much of the way we all act and react at work is habitual and subconscious, I knew that an activity allowing all of the employees in a department to participate in a non-threatening, fun, and eye-opening exercise that brought their habits to light in the form of the *Ten Levels of Workplace Disillusionment* made a lot of sense.

Such a game would need to be introduced and taught to groups of employees for it to be effective. *The Game* would also have to be embraced by management, so must be introduced to the employees in a way that demonstrates a mutual advantage to the workers and the company; no fear, no ulterior motives, no hype. To fully "wrap" this game into the most dynamic format possible, I developed *The Vocational Shrink Communications Training Program*. The *Ten Levels* grew to become a business tool; a vehicle to open up awareness of counterproductive behaviors, evaluate their sources, deal with their effects, and realize the many benefits of improved productivity, morale and, most importantly, return on investment, for participating clients.

I experimented with the first few levels writing both an "Employee Perspective" and a "Management Perspective" for each, attempting to look at each perspective through the other's eyes. Is it wise for a manager to gain a more complete understanding of the specifics of an employee's thought processes and instinctive reactions that lead to his limitations and level of disillusionment? Will an employee benefit from reading about a manager's possible strategies in dealing with staff personality types and overcoming the disillusionment? My feeling is that the *Ten Levels* will be most effective as a tool for business if engaged in openly and proactively by both managers and employees. If either of them disengages, stands aloof, makes excuses or cops out from honestly looking at themselves, the program will ultimately be less effective.

Encouraging this level of staff/management interaction adds a deeper dimension to this tool and makes understanding the *Ten Levels* concepts easier, more thorough, and will ultimately lead to better results for both employees and managers. The better each of them understands the *Ten Levels*, the more Chapter 2, "Some Common Trends" will make sense. The more they embrace the reality of the trends, the more motivated they will be to "Get Off the Merry-Go-Round" (see Chapter 3) and go on to share in a workplace that is more exciting, friendly, empowering, productive and profitable. This is the win-win-win situation that all organizations yearn for, but so often find to be elusive.

As you study the *Ten Levels of Workplace Disillusionment* – as an employee, a manager or perhaps both – you will gain the ability to identify symptoms of negative behavior patterns, confront them with confidence, and move beyond them to make your work life more enjoyable. You will be properly equipped to share these insights with your coworkers, so that everyone who chooses to will benefit from the synergy that can take the group higher together than any of you could travel alone.

Life is full of situations that, while serious in themselves, can be better comprehended and openly addressed, if looked at from the humorous side. America's first First Lady, Martha Washington, said, "The greater part of our happiness or misery depends on our dispositions, and not on our circumstances. We carry the seeds of one or the other about with us in our minds wherever we go." A lighthearted, open-minded, positive attitude makes evaluation and growth a much more pleasant, fun and rewarding activity. So here's to the understanding of our occupational oddities. Remember, if your job makes you kind of crazy, you're normal!

> *"The greater part of our happiness or misery depends on our dispositions, and not on our circumstances. We carry the seeds of one or the other about with us in our minds wherever we go."*
>
> —Martha Washington,
> America's first First Lady

> "The secret of life isn't what happens to you, but what you do with what happens to you."
>
> —Norman Vincent Peale,
> Protestant preacher and author of
> The Power of Positive Thinking

Chapter 1
The Ten Levels of Workplace Disillusionment

The workplace is an exciting arena filled with every kind of person, attitude, lifestyle and skill level imaginable. In studying them all, from the least skilled blue collar to the highest-qualified white collar, a variety of habits and recurring patterns appear as these men and women deal with the idiosyncrasies and corporate politics present in the work environment.

One of the most interesting aspects of analyzing their traits is the realization that individuals in all echelons of power practice these survival skills to some extent. While managers may choose different levels and behavioral devices than their subordinates, the constant eye toward performance reviews and future promotions causes them all to scurry into their favorite "levels" for relief and safety. These counterproductive reactions to workplace stress can lead to limited cooperation and selfish, protectionist attitudes.

Not only did I come to recognize these reactive trends, but also to realize that many of the ways particular individuals behaved were subconscious, habit-driven responses that varied by personality type—and were totally below their conscious awareness.

Norman Vincent Peale taught, "The secret of life isn't what happens to you, but what you do with what happens to you." In the workplace what people do with what happens is often a reaction, almost an instinct, based on deeply-seated habits they're unaware are controlling them. After years of observation, research and more careful analysis, what started out as a fun and harmless game of identifying and cataloging the unique reactions of fellow employees became the progressive *Ten Levels* list. Moreover, three things became obvious:

1. Employees progressed up the levels over time.

2. Personality type, age and education had the most effect on which levels a person chose and how long they stayed there.

3. All of this was well below their conscious level of thinking. These were habit patterns and reactions – not well-thought-out choices.

These observations about working people and their characteristics have been incorporated into the *Ten Levels of Workplace Disillusionment*. While the identification and classification of these behaviors have had me and colleagues rolling on the floor more than a few times, and demonstrated that the *Ten Levels* have a decidedly humorous, "human" side, we're actually dealing with some very serious issues for both workers and employers. During 20+ years building a career in the employee recognition and motivation business, I've gathered the insights and experiences that have resulted in this book.

Not all employees take on the characteristics described in the *Ten Levels of Workplace Disillusionment*. There are many jobs where people are competent, truly appreciated, and manifest that respect and trust in highly productive, rewarding careers. However, there are still a number of companies where employees are left on their own to find their individual way to happiness, motivation and success. The probability of the *Ten Levels* being present, and the magnitude of the symptoms, is directly related to the amount of autocratic management and job stress within a given workplace.

Part of the research for this book was gathered while working for a large manufacturing company as an Industrial Engineer, then later for a family-owned, but internationally known, small business. From these experiences and other evidence, I believe the *Ten Levels* may be more pronounced in a small, privately held company environment. Still, throughout the corporate world, the politics and coat-tailing required to survive at any job where you work for someone else can bring about these reactive and destructive characteristics to varying degrees.

This book by no means intends to paint a picture of all working people ultimately withering away in a downward spiral of occupational hopelessness. Quite the contrary, my goal is to open up the dark corners and shine a light on the devastating, potentially permanent damage that can be done to both employees, and the companies they work for, if the causes and effects of the *Ten Levels* are not dealt with effectively.

Examining these issues will lead to some of the ways you can counteract and overcome these inefficient and demotivating behaviors, once they are identified. This includes re-evaluation and modification of habits, changing attitudes, rethinking beliefs, and accessing available resources. That may sound like a lot to tackle, but as Dr. Gary McKay, author of 12 books including *How You Feel is Up to You*, reminds us, "…you can't change the effect past influences had on you once, you can only change the effect they have on you now." The more that management and staff can open the lines of communication regarding the causes and effects of workplace frustration, the sooner they can both begin to make the subtle changes necessary to reduce stress, increase cooperation, and greatly improve productivity and satisfaction. Isn't that the winning combination we're all looking for?

The Ten Levels of Workplace Disillusionment introduces a sequence of easy-to-recognize behavior patterns that can be used to identify reactive survival tactics that employees fall into unknowingly. Once you can distinguish the effect, you can then match it up with a cause. When both the cause and effect are open on the table, you are free to operate on the underlying problem, bandage up the wounds, and begin to enjoy the fruits of healing.

Employees can be fully utilized, self actualized and highly productive, while employers can maximize the

Chapter One

return on their investment of salaries, benefits and training. Both will be happier, healthier and will create a better company to share with others. Novelist George Eliot put it this way: "What do we live for if not to make the world less difficult for each other?"

While gathering this material, I came across some of the most unusual symptoms you can imagine, and they all represent real people and events. Sure, I had some fun and embellished a few of the identifiable symptoms a little, but not so much as to change the relevance of what we observed. I wanted to offer simple, understandable, often funny, but always real, examples of the natural, instinctive reactions of employees when put in a frustrating, demoralizing or fearful environment. As my observations and scribbled notes began to fall into predictable order and repeatable patterns, the *Ten Levels of Workplace Disillusionment* was born.

Over the past 20 years, having moved from an employee who personally experienced many of the levels, to a Recognition Consultant helping companies improve employee motivation and morale, I have grown and fine tuned the *Ten Levels* into a form that I'm confident can help both employees and their managers begin to improve their workplaces. My hope is that the awareness of the *Ten Levels of Workplace Disillusionment*, and the fresh understanding of the many ways they can reduce the effectiveness of a workforce, will help to make life at work more fun, rewarding and profitable.

The Ten Levels of Workplace Disillusionment

Level 1 – Disbelief
That stage where the initial naïveté of the new employee gives way to the questions, concerns and confusion of illogical corporate politics.

Level 2 – Nodding and Agreeing
The "don't rock the boat" stage – where the confused and/or spineless congregate to brown nose and avoid the frustration of conflicting policies.

Level 3 – Griping and Complaining
Similar to Level 1 (but now you know it's really true).
The level where the motivated achievers reside while attempting to progress and find their place in the organization.

Level 4 – Escape
Similar to Level 2, but using crutches such as drugs or alcohol to handle the frustration, rather than sacrificing one's integrity by becoming a wimp (although the long-term emotional results may be the same).

Level 5 – Gut Check
Characterized by internal physiological complications, such as backaches, ulcers and other intestinal distress.

Level 6 – Class Clown
Includes over-reaction and other bizarre behaviors, usually to counteract Level 3, or hide Level 5 symptoms.

Level 7 – Apathy
The much-envied level of the aging executive who can see the light of retirement at the end of the tunnel (can also exist in a younger person who feels overlooked and taken for granted, but this is rarer).

Level 8 – Decline and Surrender
Distinguished by external physiological complications brought on by the failed attempt to maintain Level 7.

Level 9 – Paranoia
Incessant whining and fretting due to burnout and mental decline.

Level 10 – Insanity
The ultimate conclusion to the career of the worker who avoids the stagnation of Levels 2 and 4, works past Level 6, fails to maintain Level 7, and survives Levels 8 and 9.

Chapter One •

 Level 1 — Disbelief

Most of us start out a new job with great enthusiasm and high expectations. As company politics and unexpected employee interactions begin to attract our attention, Level 1 symptoms are likely to set in. We quickly become irritated at the glaring inconsistencies we see (and everyone else doesn't seem to notice), but we just can't believe that what we are witnessing is for real.

Level 1 lasts from one week to as long as six months. The average employee, however, moves on to Level 2 in about four to six weeks, due to mental fatigue and subconscious survival instinct.

Level 1 symptoms include:

- Shaking head from side to side
- Sighing, rolling one's eyes or looking upwards
- Questioning others repeatedly about a project
- Saying "I just can't believe it" a lot

So this is Level 1. Welcome to the Real World of Work!

...meet Cindy

Cindy graduated from Northwestern just last May and couldn't wait to take on her new responsibilities in the accounting department with Randaletti Technology, Inc. (RTI). During her first 30 days on the job, she eagerly gathered basic knowledge about the company and learned the names of almost everybody on the 3rd floor of the C-1 building. As a Cum Laude accounting graduate, she had all the knowledge she needed to immediately contribute to the company's bottom line, but blending in wasn't quite as easy as she thought it was going to be.

Fran had handled payroll since 1972 and had a funny way of calculating vacation time. Although Cindy had just aced a class that gave her several new ways to computerize this process and make it easier and fairer for both full and part-time employees, Fran, for some reason, didn't embrace her suggestions.

Cindy also had trouble getting comfortable with Dan, the CFO. Although he was always friendly and helpful, her education and constant enthusiasm seemed to threaten him. He spent too much time justifying his position and qualifications, she felt, and was unwilling to give her any really juicy assignments that were up to her level of talent and capability.

Within 90 days, Cindy was beginning to question (in disbelief) many things about the company. What she had been taught in college did not help her in dealing with the people she had to work with, or the systems that often appeared to be anything but state-of-the-art. She quickly learned that it was not a good idea to go over her boss's head in voicing her concerns. Whenever she did, her boss Fran became agitated and Fran's boss Dan just smiled and told her to work it out within the department. Cindy is a classic Level 1 at this stage of her career.

Chapter One

Employee Perspective

If you're reading this as a true Level 1 (Disbelief), you are at a place where most of us have traveled before. Why? A lot has to do with our educational system. Until you get into a Masters or Doctorate program, most, if not all, of your instructors have little or no actual industry experience. They tend to be scholastic achievers who find their passion in teaching.

There is certainly nothing wrong with that; as a matter of fact, we all have stories about the wonderful teachers who shaped our visions, energized our hopes and made our dreams seem achievable. None of us would be where we are today without these wonderful, caring and dedicated professionals guiding our educational life.

The problem is, they have no knowledge or experience with corporate politics; so even if they wanted to, they can offer us no help in this area. There is also pressure on teachers to cover a defined curriculum each semester. This leads to the goal of imparting knowledge and grading tests, with little time left to consider applications in the real world.

That's why when you graduate from college you go through "commencement", a word that means "to begin." You now have amassed a large amount of disassociated knowledge and possess a written credential. This is your ticket to the real world of work where you can "commence" to learn about all of the stress, politics, frustrations, coat tailing and other adventures that make human relations in the workplace so challenging. A fascination with this aspect of work life can also lead to the opportunity to not only overcome these challenges for yourself, but also to participate in making them better for yourself and others. Later, we'll get to how you can move beyond "Disbelief".

Management Perspective

Level 1 (Disbelief) employees are a two-edged sword for you as a supervisor. Their naivety can be burdensome from a productivity and initiative point of view; however, they have not been in the working world long enough to develop deep-seated negative habit patterns, so they can prove to be the easiest to bring into a more cooperative, motivated and team-player environment. As you begin to work with your employees to bring the *Ten Levels* to light in your workplace, it is the Level 1 folks who may be the most willing to get on board. While they don't have the experience and have not yet earned the respect of the department (something that can only come with time), they tend to be the most flexible people to work with when it comes to change and trying new ideas.

Because they are still fresh, green, and open, these Level 1 (Disbelief) employees are usually the most eager to bend, because being involved, accepted and appreciated is very important to them. Use them wisely to build a base of enthusiasm, confidence and excitement in your new *Ten Levels*-based initiatives, as others who are far more entrenched in their chosen levels will prove to be much harder to awaken and get on board.

As a manager you also have the advantage of being able to step back and view the various levels in your department from a distance. You will find that a macro view of the *Ten Levels* that reside there will be invaluable as you consider how each employee needs to be coaxed into acknowledging his or her favorite hiding places. Employees will feed off of each other's newly-acquired awarenesses and can serve to make the transition to a more productive and rewarding environment easier for everyone.

Chapter One •

Level 2 —
Nodding and Agreeing

After sufficient frustration, the weary Level 1 participant unwittingly slips into Level 2. The mind shuts down a little, and chooses not to make waves—to just go with the flow for a while. Nodding and agreeing may last from one day to forever—in direct proportion to backbone dimensions. While offering a slight reprieve from the anxiety of Level 1, Level 2 has its own obvious downfall to all of us with any desire to achieve something with our lives.

Level 2 symptoms include:

- Difficulty making or maintaining eye contact
- An amazing talent for talking in circles
- Reluctance to accept responsibility
- Slumped shoulders

If you're observant, you can see experienced Level 2's nodding and agreeing about some really illogical things. You and your friends can have hours of fun getting well entrenched Level 2's to contradict themselves and agree to all kinds of counterproductive proposals. It is pathetic what an experienced Level 2 will do to avoid responsibility and controversy.

Although seemingly harmless, a cornered Level 2 will backstab, lie, and fight to maintain his or her space. Many Level 2's are at their peak of the "Peter Principle"[1] defined level of incompetence and are easily threatened. Companies with over-promoted Level 2's in upper management positions find it difficult to let themselves implement the

---

1 Dr. Laurence J. Peter's famed Peter Principle states that: "Everyone rises to their level of incompetence." Put another way: Everyone rises to at least one level above that at which they are competent.

knowledge of subordinate specialists that could be used to outdistance the competition.

"Reinventing the wheel" and long, drawn-out justifications are common within this type of leadership structure. Underutilization of employees, higher-than-average turnover and, ultimately, more costly health insurance premiums often follow.

...say hello to Ray

Ray has been with RTI for 29 years and has seen the company grow from a small subcontract shop to a multi-billion-dollar manufacturer of specialty parts for the aircraft and computer industries. He began his career working with Bob Randaletti, the Founder and President of RTI, back in Minneapolis when they both got hired on at 3M right out of college.

Ray used to be the Director of Manufacturing and has an office full of plaques and awards celebrating his achievements. He is now Director of the Composites Group, one of six production lines in the company.

Two years ago, RTI hired an MBA from a Chicago

high-tech firm, as VP of Manufacturing, to bring the company into a fully computerized, numerically controlled machine shop with direct PC control, automatic scheduling and a networked database linking all production processes.

While Ray has a tremendous amount of experience, a corner office, a first row covered parking spot, a club membership (with a locker two down from Bob), and a block of c ompany NBA season tickets at his disposal, he has become more and more quiet and complacent recently. He never misses an opportunity to be seen nodding and agreeing with Bob and makes sure that he plays the part of his biggest fan. But Bob is less accessible than he used to be. While always pleasant, he has a lot more managers and vendors to deal with than he did 20 years ago when he and Ray ran everything together.

Ray knows all the tricks about how to stay involved and look essential without taking on any more responsibility than necessary or risk shining a light on his lack of current technical expertise. Unfortunately, Bob is oblivious to the dilemma his friend is facing. There are younger employees with more up-to-date computer manufacturing credentials who the company could put in charge of the Composites Group, but no one is about to recommend that to Bob. His connections to Ray are too well known, and Bob still thinks Ray is really making things happen out there.

As Ray gets closer to retirement, he may be able to casually slide into Level 7 (Apathy); and then ride out his final years. But right now, Ray has to keep Bob on his side and appear to have his finger on the pulse of the corporation as protection from a further demotion within the department. He knows there are more qualified candidates for the new, high-tech manufacturing processes that RTI is moving into rapidly, but as long as Bob has faith in Ray, and he can keep up the look of departmental control, he is pretty safe.

While sometimes embarrassed by his Level 2 status, Ray has too much to lose by letting down the facade. He knows he can't gain the knowledge needed to keep up with the younger engineers with shiny new degrees and a lifetime of computer skills. He is also well aware that he could never change jobs and get anywhere near the salary, title and perks that he enjoys at RTI. Best to just lay low, enjoy the fruits of his labors and keep his image going as long as possible.

Employee Perspective

As a Level 2 (Nodding and Agreeing), you are one of two types of people. Most likely you are a new Level 2, fresh out of Level 1 (Disbelief) and just resting for a spell while you process all of the new information you recently gained about life in the Real World of Work.

Good news! You still have many options, such as riding out Level 2 for awhile and using the time to collect and process a few career scenarios from a position of comfort and safety. Soon, you will be compelled to jump back into the game as a virgin Level 3 (Griping and Complaining)—perhaps when an exciting-enough growth opportunity makes itself available.

If you are not coming into Level 2 for the first time, then you may be more like our friend Ray, above, who is using

Level 2 to protect his position and buy time. While self preservation is an instinctive behavior, Level 2 is not where you ultimately want your instincts to take you. This is the realm of the weak, who rely on old relationships and calling in favors to sustain themselves.

I know I'm pretty hard on long term Levels 2's, but if you find yourself here, take heart—it's still not too late. Remember, you have the advantage of experience and a better understanding of your company than most others, so you have more options to consider. By becoming part of the new interactive team and helping others identify and change their status within the *Ten Levels*, you too will be inspired and invigorated. Rather than use the past to defend your value, be a part of the new direction and you will rise to the top again.

Management Perspective

Where your Level 1 (Disbelief) employees will be the easiest to get on the team, your longest practicing Level 2 (Nodding and Agreeing) folks may be the toughest. A long-term Level 2 is in denial and probably somewhat unaware of how he or she is perceived by fellow employees, especially the younger ones. Because they can be seen as sell-outs, living off of past glory, long-term Level 2s's are not appealing role models to the younger people.

This is reality, but not an insurmountable problem. If you can get a Level 2 actively involved in your department transformation, they are able to both save face and begin to use their vast experience and latent talents in ways they have not recently considered. You stand to salvage a Level 2 (Nodding and Agreeing) victim from continuing down the slippery slope, while at the same time benefiting from their leadership with some of your younger Level 1 (Disbelief), Level 3 (Griping and Complaining), and even some new Level 4's (Escape), if they haven't progressed too far.

Level 3 — Griping and Complaining

Ahh, Level 3—by far, the most popular level of the working class. It's like Level 1 (Disbelief) in appearance, but with the important contrast that you know and accept the fact that some of your worst expectations are really occurring all around you.

Sure you could quit, but the money's pretty good and what if you couldn't find another job or the new one is as bad as this one? And what about the stock options, the profit sharing, the insurance, blah, blah, blah . . . This is the notable thought pattern of Level 3, which keeps you frustrated enough to resort to griping and moaning as ventilation therapy. Strong Level 3's are most prevalent in family businesses and other heavily bureaucratic organizations that tend to use overpaying as the only meaningful form of employee recognition.

Most of a company's young, enthusiastic new employees bound quickly past Level 2 (Nodding and Agreeing), only to spend the majority of their career in Level 3 (Griping and Complaining), looking for fulfillment and recognition. Unfortunately, the strongest Level 3's are also the employees who are most likely to leave one day and start their own business, or go to a competitor that better motivates and utilizes its people.

It is remarkably easy to get sucked into the lamentations of your local "gripe groups" or "bitch bunches" around the water cooler or lunchroom to let off a little steam, where you'll hear "…so and so did such and such . . . they'll get theirs!" Then they calmly get on with their day. Be careful, though, because as you will soon find out, these seemingly harmless groups often house the company's Level 9's (Paranoia), and these guys and gals are not only very demotivating, but are at the risk of going Level 10 (Insanity) at any time (read on!).

Chapter One

Level 3 symptoms include:
- High frustration levels
- Territory dominance
- Frequent use of "if only…" statements
- Random threats to partake of Level 4 activities

…when Sheldon *met* Christine

Sheldon and Christine both came to RTI from successful careers with other manufacturing companies. They have 12 and 9 years of experience respectively, and know all the ins and outs of corporate survival. They each hit the ground running in middle management at RTI, but soon found out that the depth and competence of their staffs and superiors were not all that they were cracked up to be.

Sheldon's Quality Control department is critical to the profitability of every production line in the plant, but he is forever fighting to get approval on new testing equipment available to more accurately measure tight tolerance milling operations. Sure, the existing devices work, but he has presented several formal proposals showing cost savings of 15 to 20 percent per year in improved setup times and reduced scrap. It always comes down to budget concerns controlled by supervisors too far removed, it seems, to appreciate the importance of his concerns. At least that's what their lack of response tells him.

Christine's call center takes upwards of 1,000 information requests and phone orders per day. She has successfully cut costs and improved response time without additional staff for the past two years, but now is struggling to add three more, well-justified, technical support people. Although Christine's thoroughly researched and professionally written proposal was immediately approved by her boss, it is bogged down in a newly formed budget committee that is considering outsourcing both her call center and the company's mailroom to a very competitively priced vendor. She is familiar with that particular vendor from her previous job, but is finding it difficult to convince management that, while they may be able to handle the mail room function, RTI would be better off keeping internal control over the phones. Her rationale regarding both service and security is well founded, but again her proposal falls to the distant and unresponsive budget committee for approval.

Sheldon and Christine have begun to share each other's frustrations, griping and complaining in impromptu discussions during breaks. They can sometimes even be coaxed into various "grumble gatherings" and "threaten throngs" to vent some of their disapproval for the way that management is holding up progress for the company. Both of these employees are on the fast track with RTI, but often find their enthusiasm curtailed by policies and slow, bureaucratic committees that they see as doing nothing more than making an already tough job even harder.

They are classic Levels 3's, at constant risk of losing ground to the disconnection of Level 4 (Escape), the discomfort of Level 5 (Gut Check), the temporary relief of Level 6 (Class Clown), or even the panacea of Level 7 (Apathy) over time.

Perhaps they will be able to convince an overly vertical management structure to allow increased lower level decision-making in certain areas. They might be able to infiltrate some of the newly formed committees, so their ideas can be more readily heard. Hopefully, they will become part of the solution, rather than part of the problem, by keeping their cool and working with management to improve the work environment within their circle of influence.

Employee Perspective

While it is probably becoming obvious to you already that none of the *Ten Levels* represent healthy places to spend your career, Level 3 (Griping and Complaining) is by far the most promising place to find yourself. It means you still have a burning desire to achieve success. You are a dedicated employee with determination, pride and the grit to keep plugging away. The periodic ventilation therapy you partake of is a way of letting off a little steam, so you can get back to work. The danger lies in the tendency for these bouts of shared frustration to become a habit, robbing you of productive time and draining your energy.

Because a department's Level 3's are often also its leaders, you are probably one of the people most likely to spearhead the introduction of the *Ten Levels* to your fellow employees. The good news is, the time and interest you put into sharing the *Ten Levels*, and helping others to become aware of their habits, will reduce some of the time spent griping and complaining. That's the secret to survival in Level 3; you are constantly on the lookout for intriguing, new challenges to get you pumped up again. The beauty of the *Ten Levels* is that this exercise can have a lasting impact on you, your associates, and your managers. If you participate in helping others—as well as yourself—identify and escape your levels, the results will be a permanently improved workplace with more productivity, opportunity, and fun – just what Level 3's (or better said, ex-Level 3's) will thrive on!

Management Perspective

Your department's Level 3's are usually the most active, demanding and creative folks, so they will naturally be the first people you will look to for reactions to this type of communications training. The longer they have been hanging out in Level 3 (Griping and Complaining), the more likely they will initially be pessimistic about *Ten Levels*. However, it is their need to be productive and moving ahead with their career – ambition is their soft spot. If you can hook them with the benefits, get them to participate in developing departmental goals. If you win them over to the long-term benefits for themselves, as well as the company, they'll help you rally the rest of the troops. Get these folks on your team and they'll row the boat for you, allowing you to spend valuable time in your macro mode, viewing the department as a whole during the transition.

Because communications training can be used as a non-threatening way for opening people up to the wasteful ways of their favorite levels, it can give you the opportunity to periodically break up a "gripe group" and finesse the Level 3's back into action. Remember, all of the levels are habits, so even the most well-meaning employees will backslide from time to time. The beauty of training-based communications training is that everyone buys into the objectives, so they can't fight too hard when their Level 3 behavior is later pointed out.

I suggest you take it easy on Level 3's with regards to pointing out their griping and complaining behaviors. These kinds of people pride themselves on self discipline and you'll find they won't need to be reminded often to think positively and remember the big picture. These are the future leaders of this company, along with you, so remind yourself that you are better off working with them than against them. Many a frustrated Level 3 who leaves their current company, comes back as a competitor; if so, they'll be out to get you with a vengeance and they're armed with a whole lot of knowledge about your weaknesses! Best to win these people over and work with them to make all of their roles more rewarding right there at your company.

Level 4 — Escape

Here's a tricky level. Many of your friends, even people in your favorite "beef bevy," are disguised Level 3's (Griping and Complaining), slowly slipping into Level 4, and they probably aren't even aware of it. The pressures of Level 3 are simply too tough for the average person to cope with for extended periods of time. Drinking (or other mind-numbing options) starts out as a social activity, but can change into a habit, often in proportion to the amount of frustration one has felt combined with a person's "tolerance" or threshold for dependency.

Those harmless trips to the local pub for a beer are the breeding ground of Level 4 mentality. Be particularly wary if those trips begin to occur before work or during lunch. In many cases, particularly in a social setting, Level 4's seem a lot like Level 9's (Paranoia). The difference is, a Level 4 still has a realistic chance to pull out of it, while a true Level 9 is only going to be helped by extensive therapy, and unfortunately, their acceptance of professional help is rare.

Level 4 symptoms include:
- Reminiscing about childhood experiences
- A short (or shorter) fuse
- Making mistakes out of haste or carelessness
- Getting a Mohawk

Not all Level 3's (Griping and Complaining) move on to Level 4 for relief. How nice to know, you may be saying. The rest of us can look forward to crawling through Levels 5 (Gut Check) and 6 (Class Clown) to the potential tranquility of Level 7 (Apathy).

Chapter One

...you know Chris in Shipping

Chris has been in the shipping and receiving area as long as anyone can remember. As one of Mr. Randaletti's first group of employees hired as the business began to grow, Chris really knows the inner workings of RTI.

As an early department head, much of the credit for breaking shipping records was given to Chris. This was an employee with an unlimited future, maybe not as a designer or engineer, but as a top performer in the production and distribution end of the business. Chris was always willing to lend a hand, and took part in many of the company's extracurricular activities. Captain of the darts team, top bowler with a 200+ average, scrappy pitcher for the softball team and the best setter the RTI volleyball team ever had.

All of these events ended with harmless trips to the local bars in the area. As the years went by, Chris began to slide into a regime involving more frequent and longer lasting bar (escape) visits. After work is a given. During lunch…well, more often than anybody knows. That goal of quitting smoking never quite happened. After 15 years, this lifestyle is beginning to take its toll. Don't get me wrong, Chris is still a hard working and dedicated employee, but that "Johnny on the spot" attitude has diminished. That early morning reliability has dragged into an 8:45 to 4:30 schedule. Age has crept up and begun to show the accumulated signs of the physical abuse and inconsistent sleep patterns.

Because of his time with the company and unquestioned skill, it is tough for management to confront Chris' slow decline, however it is becoming a point of discussion during annual reviews. A Level 4 can be turned around but, as with any addictive habit pattern, it must begin with the victim's acknowledgement of the disease and a true desire to change. Hopefully, for RTI and Chris, this will happen before declining health makes it too late to turn back.

Employee Perspective

Let's be honest; nobody plans to slip into chemical dependency. Obviously, many people have not been as successful as they'd like in their attempts to avoid this stress-induced dilemma. Like any addiction, the first and most important step is to admit it, so here's your chance. If your employer has provided you with formal communications training, you probably have one of the best possible scenarios to courageously and candidly address your status and make the changes needed to get your life and work back on track.

Because of the number of different chemicals that make

up Level 4 behavior, and the fact that everyone handles these things differently, our goal is not to pigeonhole symptoms or suggest a blanket diagnosis. This is a personal issue and will be dealt with only when you are ready. All I can say with certainty is that you have a better chance of succeeding in your attempt to battle this disease (or habit that could lead to a disease) and keep your job, if you confront it in the context of *The Ten Levels*.

Most Level 4's are actually Level 3's (Griping and Complaining) that got sidetracked during one of their runs around the 3-6 Loop (Cyclic Trends). This means that you were probably a valuable, highly functional asset to your firm before your slide and that you can easily become that kind of employee again. Most people root for the underdog and besting chemical dependency, as common as it is in our society, and it's one of the places that carries forgiveness and congratulations to those who are fortunate enough to recover.

Management Perspective

As important as it is for human beings to help one another, your role in rescuing your Level 4 employees carries with it a multiple benefit. Sure, it would give you a feeling of pride and accomplishment to participate in helping anyone beat an addiction but, as we mentioned above, many Level 4's began as valuable, productive employees.

Early stage Level 4's are a worthy and realistic group for you to help as a manager. You get to enjoy the dual blessing of saving a friend from a declining downward spiral and, if you are successful, you also get an experienced, quality employee who will make an immediate positive contribution to your department. It is likely that they will actually come back even stronger, having skirted the edge of disaster. These people have the potential to lead others, both by example and through their fresh enthusiasm. You are wielding some great power here, because these Level 4's are usually pretty popular folks and carry a lot of others in their wake.

The danger, of course, is that some Level 4's are simply not salvageable, so you are taking a chance. I don't know if there is a way to estimate the possibility of bringing a borderline Level 4 back, however, I strongly believe that using communications training as a way of getting their attention and offering them a safe vehicle maximizes your odds of success. While no substitute for professional help, it's definitely worth a try, as the alternative is obvious and inevitable.

Chapter One

Level 5 — Gut Check

Level 5, the mystery level. Generally, you aren't aware that your buddy is a Level 5 unless he or she tells you. Level 5 introduces annoyances like: Lower back aches, indigestion, ulcers, high blood pressure, rapid heart rate, and other intestinal aches and pains not easily distinguishable by your Level 3 (Griping and Complaining) peers (who may be Level 5's too, for all you know).

Level 5 symptoms include:

- That glassy eyed look of uncertainty as in, "I've already gone four times this morning, but I just might need another trip . . ."
- Lack of motivation
- Reduced interest in tackling new challenges
- Holding stomach (or side) and wincing

Obviously, an individual's pain threshold dictates how long they can remain in Level 5 while keeping everyone else convinced they're still as much a Level 3 as ever. The damage is done either way and soon the mind succumbs to the discomfort. On to Level 6 (Class Clown), you lucky thing you!

• The Ten Levels of Workplace Disillusionment

...superwoman Gwen

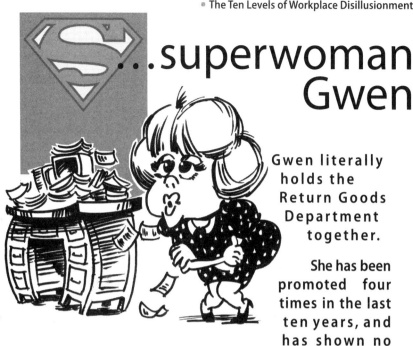

Gwen literally holds the Return Goods Department together.

She has been promoted four times in the last ten years, and has shown no signs of shrinking from any new challenge. While occasionally succumbing to the allure of Level 3 (Griping and Complaining) "put-down posses," Gwen has been a model employee in this fast-paced, high growth corporation.

Recently, Gwen has been having some stomach symptoms that have caught her by surprise. The workload and stress don't seem to have increased, but her energy level just isn't what it used to be. Maybe it's the coffee, or the infrequent, less-than-nutritious meals, grabbed on the run, but she is going through more TUMS® than normal and is experiencing more frequent bouts of intestinal rebellion.

No one seems to notice the difference. Gwen is so good at what she does, and has such a strong work ethic, that she handles the inconvenience of these new gut check challenges without missing a beat. Because her performance and attitude remain strong, she is able to continue on without attracting any management attention. This is the beginning of Level 5 (Gut Check) for Gwen, and it will only get worse if not attended to soon.

The normal pattern, if she doesn't change her work habits, will be increased internal discomfort, additional medications, less energy and, ultimately, a decline in performance. Along the way, she will constantly be at risk of sliding into the mental vacation of Level 6 (Class Clown) and beginning a series of 3-6 Loops (Cyclic Trends). As a 3-6 Looper, she then inherits the potential of taking a permanent escape to Level 4, or giving up to the tranquility of Level 7 (Apathy).

Hard working Level 5's like Gwen need to be handled just like Level 3's (Griping and Complaining), because they are often indistinguishable from them. They maintain the same dedicated, aggressive and professional tendencies that have made them successful, but are at greater risk of falling prey to other dangers within the system, once the Level 5 symptoms begin to eat away at their concentration and resilience.

Management's ability to identify and work with the Level 3's and Level 5's in their organization will have immediate impact on productivity and morale throughout the entire staff. These people represent the leaders and motivators of your company, and the others will tend to respond to their guidance. By nature, they are also the most responsive to new opportunities and changes that simplify the systems that so often restrict their growth.

Employee Perspective

The ball is really in your court here, as a new Level 5. You have probably had conflicting thoughts about the increased frequency and intensity of your intestinal symptoms, but may well have been able to hide them from your other Level 3 coworkers (Griping and Complaining). I can guarantee you this, however; you can't win this one by ignoring it and covering it up.

Early Level 5 annoyances are your wake-up call that the stress of Level 3 (Griping and Complaining), is beginning to take its toll. If you are new to Level 5, then this material has gotten into your hands at just the right time, because you can simply follow the previous Level 3 advice and nobody will be the wiser. Not that there is any embarrassment to the confrontation of physical limitations but depending on your age, you may just not want to be seen in that group yet.

If you are farther along in your Level 5 journey and are already well schooled in the use of various over-the-counter remedies, then you'll have to consider more serious life-changing decisions. I would venture to guess that your diet and exercise routine is not as it should be, your weight and blood pressure may not be optimal, and you may just not give a darn! Go ahead… vent, justify, make whatever excuses your need to, and when you're done, a quality training solution will be waiting . . . !

Okay, ready to listen now? Here's the deal; no matter what kind of shape you are in or have ever been in, it is an undisputed fact that getting a handle on your food and beverage intake and getting your body in some semblance of shape will do wonders in combating the stress demons that are eating your insides. It's not going to go into a full health and fitness program discussion here, but will make three points and one suggestion:

1. Cardiovascular exercise (anything that takes your heart rate up to a minimum of 60% of your Maximum Heart Rate for 20 to 30 minutes at a time three to four times a week is a great way to get your circulatory system in shape.

2. Weight lifting that works individual muscle groups to a point of exhaustion will break down muscle

tissue and allow it to rebuild larger and stronger. Muscle is where the enzymes that control metabolism live, so the more "lean muscle mass" you have, the more efficiently your body burns calories all the time.

3. What you eat and drink, and when you do it is the secret to the whole thing. The word "DIET" is a bad word (anything with the word "DIE" in it can't be too uplifting!), but what it actually refers to is "What You Eat". Add to that "When You Eat" and "What you Drink" and you are there.

I have a wonderful story about my own fitness journey that I'm saving for my next book, but I will suggest this resource. *Body for Life*2[2] by Bill Phillips is the best book I have read that really makes sense, seems doable, and doesn't turn you into a gym rat. As a matter of fact, the more complex and time consuming your health and fitness routine becomes, the more likely you won't stick to it . . . just like all the diets you've ever tried!

Getting a grip on your health is always a good idea, but Level 5 seems to be a particularly good time for many of us to finally take it seriously. You may be experiencing physical complications for the first time in a basically healthy life. You may also still be young enough to be willing to take a run at it. Level 8's (Decline & Surrender) are often older and have truly debilitating complications on top of the simple Level 5 stuff, so they find it harder to look realistically at fitness programs. This is the stage in your life and career where you are being given the prodding you need, before irreversible problems have taken away the window of opportunity.

Level 5 is a bit of a resting place in *The Ten Levels*,

---

[2] Body for Life, Bill Philips, HarperCollins *Publishers* 1999

perhaps an unintentional one, but a change of pace, no less. It represents the perfect time in your career to honestly look at your health, your diet and exercise habits, and to consider some long-term changes. You may well look back on it as a significant turning point in your life.

Management Perspective

Next to salvaging borderline Level 4's (Escape), your best use of communications training will be in reestablishing positive, productive and healthy goals with your Level 5's. Level 3 (Griping and Complaining) and Level 5 make up the bulk of your department's employees—perhaps as much as 75 to 80 percent. Because it is often impossible to differentiate Level 5's from Level 3's, you are best to simply consider them all Level 3's until you are made aware of, or notice, the symptoms of a Level 5 ailment.

The good news is that you can keep it simple and deal with them pretty much the same way. Start out using the

Management Perspective for Level 3, then identify the Level 5's as they show themselves. Actually, the health and fitness suggestions for Level 5 will not be wasted on Level 3's, as they will be there sooner or later if they stay on the Level 3 (Griping and Complaining) track. These two levels house your greatest asset and until the Level 5 symptoms arrived, they were cut from identical cloth. As a supervisor, you are very likely to relate to these folks. This is where the aggressive, positive, motivated, take charge people cut their teeth, so you must have had some of these characteristics to have been promoted to management.

    You may find that advocating a healthy diet and exercise lifestyle, then participating along with your employees, will benefit you as much as them, while offering a way of building camaraderie and mutual respect. The two most important ingredients in good human relations are respect and genuine caring. Recommending something to your subordinates, then participating in it with them is a great way to enhance both of these goals in your workplace, and you can even incentify it to measure and prove it's worth it.

    Level 5 is the turning point in the *Ten Levels*. Level 6 (Class Clown) offers one last bastion of hope, but beyond that it becomes a slippery slope. You can burn a tremendous amount of energy and resources trying to revitalize these folks. These active, creative, proud and experienced people are your foundation to the turnaround you strive for in using these tools. Getting employees on board by Level 5 is one of the keys to maximizing the effectiveness of this program.

Level 6 — Class Clown

For some reason, the mind is subtly altered by the first five Levels of Workplace Disillusionment. Maybe it's the frustration of Levels 1, 2, and 3; the involvement, or fear of involvement, in Level 4; or the discomfort and secrecy of Level 5. It's hard to say for sure. Regardless, Level 6 becomes the "catch-all" for the slightly demented peculiarities that haunt the mind of the war weary employee after years of struggling for fulfillment in our country's factories and offices.

Level 6 symptoms include:

- A false sense of security
- A nonchalant, almost jovial attitude
- Doing imitations of fellow workers
- Mistelling old jokes and humming obscure tunes

Although Level 6's help to liven up the place, you must be cognizant of the fact that they are sensitive and should not be antagonized. Your best response is to treat them like any of your Level 3 (Griping and Complaining) buddies, unless they directly interfere with your job function. Direct confrontation could result in their transference to Level 7 (Apathy), or …gasp …beyond!

Chapter One

...Quick Wit Gene...

Gene has always had a quick wit and good sense of humor. His talent and educational credentials, with a Masters Degree in Metallurgy and 10 years of experience, have never been questioned, but lately he seems

more interested in the joke he heard the other day, or the next gag he plans to pull, than in the status of the shop's Heat Treat facilities.

Don't get me wrong – he's not out sabotaging the annealing furnaces or tripping people while they are carrying racks of hot forgings, but his attitude seems more intent on being a class clown than work. Gene is a blast to be around and is very popular at all company functions. He can do an imitation of Fred, the vacuum furnace department lead man, better than Fred can do himself!

Gene has not changed his work ethic or ability to juggle the never-ending changes and rush jobs that continually pour into his department. He just seems to have lost his intensity and the furrowed brow that was always one of his distinguishing characteristics. While no one can show evidence that this new, upbeat, almost loosy-goosy style has affected his performance, it is making some people nervous. It's almost like a different Gene, and while he is more fun to be around, there is the tendency for everyone to find themselves waiting for the other shoe to drop.

Unlike Level 5 (Gut Check), which is often undistinguishable for long periods of time, Level 6 is easy to spot. It is usually a rather big departure from the victim's normal work style, and is often loud and attention-getting. Because it is associated with fun, and is usually a stress reducer for everyone involved, Level 6 is not seen as a negative habit pattern at all. What's wrong with having a little fun at work, anyway?

The problem is, that Level 6er's have not become that way as a healthy alternative to acting too serious on the job. They have succumbed to Class Clown status as a defense against the stresses and frustrations of Level 3 (Griping and Complaining), and the inevitable discomforts of Level 5 (Gut Check). What could be seen as a positive change of attitudes is really a resting place where the bedraggled high achiever regains his or her strength until a sufficiently intriguing new project responsibility drags them back down to Level 3 (Griping and Complaining). Then, unless something has changed in company politics, the cycle begins again.

If Level 6 becomes too much fun, and a "Level 3 instigating challenge" does not present itself soon enough, our happy-go-lucky employee begins to risk falling prey to Level 7 (Apathy). As retirement approaches, experience in Level 6 can actually expedite the transition to Level 7 (Apathy). The reduced stress and free use of the imagination can make daydreams of the cabin on the lake and sipping iced tea sound more inviting than that next big project. Here is where sentient management must step in and deftly lead this droll, but misfocused, player back into the game.

This is a very critical turning point in the *Ten Levels of Workplace Disillusionment*. As you will see, once an employee enters Level 7 (Apathy), there is usually no turning back. A Level 6 can easily be coaxed back into the fray, but a true Level 7 has only retirement or Level 8 (Decline & Surrender) to look forward to.

Employee Perspective

Congratulations, you've selected one of the more fun places to rest up on the *Ten Levels of Workplace Disillusionment*. Unlike Level 5 (Gut Check), where the need for a vacation is forced upon you by bodily discomfort, Level 6 is a departure from the seriousness and stress of everyday work chosen in a somewhat brazen, "what-the-heck" manner. Although Level 6 is a choice, it is really a choice made between several evils.

You probably got here because of the stress that built up in Level 3 (Griping and Complaining), an aversion to the chemical alternatives of Level 4 (Escape) or as a way to skip experiencing Level 5 (Gut Check) symptoms. Or, perhaps it was your method for dealing with Level 5 symptoms. Either way, you're not dealing with stress in a totally healthy way, even though it tends to be more personally and socially acceptable to become the Level 6 than to self destruct or stay angry. Does that sound like you?

Going to Level 6 from Level 3 (Griping and Complaining) and back is so common that we have a name for it – the 3-6 Loop (Cyclic Trends). In other words, you're not alone!

There are some striking positives and negatives to dwelling in Level 6 for too long, so I'll describe a way to keep the good and drop the bad as you get a grip on why Level 6 is your drug of choice.

Let's face it, there's nothing wrong with a good sense of humor. The jokers and clowns make work fun and keep folks smiling; that's the good part, so don't lose that. The fact that many go there as an escape to avoid dealing with their stresses and frustrations is the negative side of this characteristic. Too much joking and playing can cause you to slip in your job performance and get to a point where you don't even care. The key here is to sort the wheat from the chaff. Use your new habit of fun-loving adventure to relax, but also remind yourself that this is just laughter therapy to help unwind and refocus on your job. Because most Level 6's are not there long term, but simply as a reprieve from job stress, it is probably the least dangerous level. However, like the other exit levels – Level 2 (Nodding and Agreeing), Level 4 (Escape), Level 7 (Apathy) and Level 9 (Paranoia) – it's easy to think you're in control and that you can quit any time you want, when you are actually getting sucked into the comfort of habit.

Have fun in Level 6 when needed, but make sure to test yourself regularly by buckling down to your work aggressively and keeping the sense of humor at the same time. This is as close as you can get to a glimpse of life outside of the *Ten Levels* before actually breaking free!

Management Perspective

The problem with your Level 6 employees is that they are just a hoot to hang out with. It is tough to be the spoiler, so management usually looks the other way, justifies them as good for the department's morale, and lives with it, as long as they don't fall into sexual harassment or some other unacceptable level of fun.

Chapter One

When you can identify a Level 5 (Gut Check), they are a sitting duck, because their intestinal discomfort slows them down and makes them ripe for talk of change. Level 6's, on the other hand, are much more elusive. They aren't really doing anything wrong and most of them are still productive, so what do you do to address this behavior?

First, remind yourself that you're probably dealing with a 3-6 Looper (Cyclic Trends), so they will be a Level 3 (Griping and Complaining) again soon. Second, be cognizant of the fact that they are now at the final "recoverable" level, so if you don't get them now before they get too close to retirement age, you risk losing them to Level 7 (Apathy). In Level 7, you'll have no choice but to just make them comfortable and keep them from infecting the rest of the troops.

I suggest you treat Level 6's just like Level 3's and simply wait for them to come around the Loop to Level 3 again. If you confront the behavior change or try to point out sags in their performance, they'll deny it and it will quickly degenerate into a "he said, she said" mode. Most Level 6's are just tired Level 3's anyway, so getting them to be part of the solution rather than dwelling on how they may be part of the problem has a much better chance of success. Success breeds success, so as you get other employees on board, your Level 6's will not only be drawn to the enthusiasm, but will make the whole game a lot more fun.

The older your Level 6, the more careful you have to be, however, because the lure of Level 7 (Apathy) and The Fulcrum (Self-Maintaining Trends) begins to compete for their attention. I suggest you keep them laughing while you subtly invite them to participate and even help lead the new vision of the department. Like Level 4 (Escape) folks, Level 6's tend to be pretty popular around the office and can bring a number of others over with them when you get them involved.

Level 7 — Apathy

Just when you were starting to consider moving to a small town in Wyoming and becoming a convenience store clerk, there's a lull in the storm. Level 7 houses the fortunate few who honestly don't care. They smile and leisurely go about their business. They tend to move in predictable patterns from day to day. Their reactions are slow, deliberate and very professional, if necessary, but without ambition and drive. Let's be reasonable – if they get too fired up, they'll risk falling back to Level 3 (Griping and Complaining)!

The problem with Level 7 is that it's incredibly hard to stay there. You sit on the fulcrum, not wanting to slide back to the 3-6 Loop (Cyclic Trends) or fall over toward a slow slide into the oblivion of Levels 8, 9 or 10.

Level 7 symptoms include:

- A relaxed, almost lazy demeanor, with an occasional noncommittal chuckle

- Avoidance of confrontation with the innate ability to look through the situation to blues skies on the horizon

- Narcolepsy

- Knowing (to the hour) how long you have until retirement

Level 7's cannot remain Level 7's for long periods of time. Most were once strong Level 3's (Griping and Complaining) and can be drawn back down periodically if tricked into assuming responsibility by shrewd management.

Chapter One

...Heeeerre's Harry!

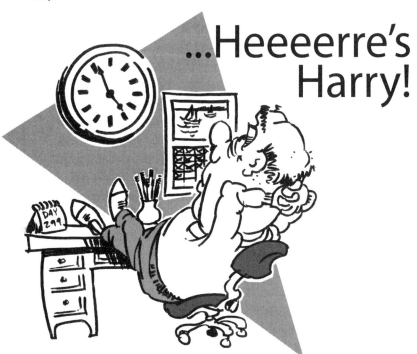

Harry is known throughout the industry as one of the most innovative product designers around. He's responsible for many of RTI's early successes, and a number of his components are still being produced for major customers. Harry has always been one of the first people in the office, and is a real team player.

Over the past couple of years, however, as new computer-aided design equipment has begun to replace the drawing boards in the department, and new blood has come in along with the new VP, Harry seems to be slowing down a little. He has always been an avid fisherman, but now his stories about the week at Lake Powell or the deep sea experience in Cabo are told with more frequency and emotion. With retirement only three years (two years, ten months, 13 days, and 2½ hours, to be exact) away, Harry's mind wanders.

He can often be seen during lunch time or breaks, thumbing through an *American Angler* magazine or looking at the current month on his Fishing Facts calendar with a glazed look and a sigh. His work is still top notch and he is about as efficient as anyone in the department, but the thrill is gone. Harry was a classic Level 3 (Griping and Complaining) during his early career, one of the best, or so it seemed, at handling the pressure of corporate politics. No one really knows how much of the last few years were spent in Level 3, and how much in Level 5 (Gut Check), but Harry has finally reached the pinnacle of his trip through the system. He was never very comfortable as a Level 6 (Class Clown), although we all remember times when he did go there for some comfort.

The combination of time, stress and pending retirement have finally taken him to a new place, a balancing act called Level 7 (Apathy). It's not that he doesn't care – Harry is a true company man who would never do anything to hurt RTI or its employees. He has just lost the grit to keep fighting new battles, and the reality of his retirement dreams are becoming more and more alluring to him now.

Similar to Ray, our Level 2 (Nodding and Agreeing) example, Harry has earned his place in upper management and is not at risk of being replaced, as long as Bob still thinks he's cutting it. The difference is that he does not fear his fate—he only has to ride out a little more time doing what he knows how to do and living off his past glory. This is a far less frightening position to be in than Level 2, however, and over time it can lead to a pretty lackadaisical attitude. No more real challenges, no more big successes or big failures either. Harry has to be careful to avoid getting too wrapped up in new projects, because he can't let himself get pulled back down into Level 3 (Griping and Complaining). It's not the excitement of a new challenge as much as it is the inevitable ride back through the discomfort of Level 5 (Gut Check) that he just can't seem to work up enough energy to confront again.

Better to just bide his time, count the days, keep it all in perspective and dream. All we can hope for is that Harry makes it to that blessed day, and has enough health and motivation left to really enjoy the realization of those dreams and his well-earned retirement. The objective is virtuous, but the odds are, unfortunately, against him as he burns up valuable vitality riding The Fulcrum (see Cyclic Trends), and avoiding the fire of Level 8 (Decline & Surrender).

Employee Perspective

You never planned to be here in Level 7, I'll bet. Interestingly enough, in the time you spend reading this sentence, you may not be there anymore! Level 7 is the peak of *Ten Levels of Workplace Disillusionment*, not Level 10 (Insanity) like you might think. Before Level 7 lie all of the grit and growth levels filled with employees striving to find their place in the workforce. Beyond Level 7 are the declining valleys from which few return. Balancing Level 7 is extremely difficult; virtually impossible for an extended period of time.

You are trying to avoid all of the frustration and stress of the first six levels (where you have spent the majority of your career) and ride out the remainder of your career, but are petrified of falling victim to Level 8 (Decline & Surrender), Level 9 (Paranoia), or Level 10 (Insanity). Good luck—you are now rolling the dice. Here are a few questions to ask yourself, if you want to take this gamble:

1. How long is it until you can retire?
2. Do you think you can actually last that long in Level 7?
3. If you can't, which way will you fall?
4. Then what???

Here's the Catch 22. If you had the strength to continue the battle, you would still be running the 3-6 Loop (Chapter 11-Cyclic Trends). If you really don't have the strength, you are at high risk of falling over into Level 8 or beyond. This is a dangerous quandary and nobody can, or wants, to help you. Not that they don't like you or care, but the truth is, everyone is secretly envious of Level 7. We all wish we could hang out there, but know it is a mine field. While one part of us hopes you can pull it off, another part of us hopes you fail so that we can feel better about our lack of courage.

If we really had any guts, we would be honest with you and suggest you go back and read the list again. Then, we'd suggest that you measure your Level 7 plan carefully and make sure you can time this final dash to freedom properly. My personal suggestion is to do everything you can to make it as short as possible, because if you fail, it will be at least emotionally draining and at most terminal!

Management Perspective

This is a tough one, however relax. You will experience few true Level 7's in your career. Even the ones that claim to be Level 7 are probably just Level 3's (Griping and Complaining) with a pipe dream, or Level 4's (Escape) who had one extra martini at lunch, maybe Level 5's (Gut Check) trying to ease the pain, or Level 6's (Class Clown) trying to fool themselves. An actual Level 7 will need to be tested over time. If and when you find a true Level 7, you owe it to them, yourself, and the rest of the department to do whatever it takes to help them make it safely (and quickly) to retirement. They have paid their dues, deserve to break free without losing face, and stand to be of no value to you in enhancing your other employees' morale or team spirit.

In the meantime, treat them like your Level 3's and 5's and see what happens. If they are going to fall out of Level 7, better for it to be back into the grind than into the abyss.

Chapter One •

You have nothing to lose and no other options until you are genuinely convinced they are an actual Level 7. Then, go to upper management and make sure they are assisted to as rapid a retirement as possible. They will benefit from having more time left to enjoy the rest of their life of leisure, you will be able to get back to more important management responsibilities, you'll be cutting costs, and your employees will avoid the needless distraction.

Level 8 — Decline and Surrender

Your Level 8 is usually a person who bounced in and out of Level 7 (Apathy) for a while and just couldn't handle the boredom. Like Level 5 (Gut Check), Level 8 involves the body responding to past frustrations and mistreatment. Level 8's often appear tired and unhealthy, and have many pills, ointments, inhalants, and lotions in their desks. Don't get a Level 8 confused with someone who actually has an allergy or skin rash, as you could blow a perfectly good diagnosis.

Level 8 symptoms include:

- Hair loss (not normal baldness, but random patches)
- Twitching, scratching, and a sickly look
- A recurring, pathetic sigh
- Fatigue

Level 8's may appear confused, because they have made the decision to move on with their careers (rather than struggle to stay in Level 7 (Apathy) when they are truly not apathetic enough to pull it off), but can't muster the energy to take another run at Level 3 (Griping and Complaining). Watch them closely – some could be handy to know. They usually have a lot of valuable experience and little to lose. If they are lucky, they will retire before having to deal with Levels 9 (Paranoia) or 10 (Insanity).

Chapter One

...meet the "nice-guy"— *Sid*

Sid is the kind of guy who you would confidently go to if you had $5,000 bucks you needed to have guarded for a week. He is calm, friendly, low key, and impeccably honest. Not any ball of fire, but reliable, fair, and with a wealth of knowledge about all aspects of the Inspection and Testing Department.

Fifteen years with NASA, then twelve more at RTI; this guy has been around a lot of pretty cool manufacturing processes and fascinating development projects in his day. A lot like our Level 7 (Apathy) friend Harry,

Sid rode the fast lane for a long time prior to slowly settling into his anticipated smooth ride to retirement.

Unfortunately, Sid was unable to properly time his final kick into Level 7 (Apathy) with his ability to handle true apathy. In the same way the go-getter Level 3 (Griping and Complaining) unwittingly slips into Level 5 (Gut Check) while nobody notices, our seemingly composed ninth-inning closer falls prey to Level 8. Unlike the internal complications of Level 5 (Gut Check), the Level 8 victim experiences more visible signs of the battle. Rashes, hair loss, and an overall sickly look often begin to take over as daily concerns. Today's medical community offers a plethora of remedies and comforts that can manage the symptoms for quite a long time, but the inevitable damage is done. That blessed retirement is being shortened, eaten away by the very institution that made it possible.

If Sid is lucky, his career will be completed before the physical limitations restrict too many of his retirement plans. Often, this is not the case. As much as everyone hopes to leave at the top of their game, it is not as easy as it seems. Higher pay, bigger responsibilities, and the realization of job opportunities only imagined earlier in their career make it hard for successful achievers to leave the system while they are still on their game. By the time the real end is near, they are left to balance the time that remains with a gnawing realization that they have passed their prime, and everyone knows it.

That may or may not be true, but if they believe it to be, their trip through Level 7 (Apathy) carries with it greater risk of the body reacting with Level 8 symptoms and a rapid slide begins. It is ironic, but the more accomplished an employee becomes during his or her career, the more difficult it is to pull off a judicious exit from the game. The same character strengths that are responsible for the past success and duration of a celebrated career make the timely and effectual acceptance of Level 7 (Apathy) more prone to failure.

This is one of the built-in dilemmas often associated with a corporate career. It can bring some of the greatest joy and pride in life, but there is not a clear-cut exit strategy available to many participants, and logic is often weaker than emotion when considering retirement options. When left too long, the system that creates an employee's success often ends up being responsible for their unflattering and early demise.

Employee Perspective

Level 8 is not a fun level, so I'll be frank with you and not joke around. You don't want to stay here long. Anyone who reaches Level 8 (Decline & Surrender) is not a spring chicken and is here for one of two reasons. Either you hit Level 7 (Apathy) too soon to ride it out all the way to retirement, or you burned out and just have more time left on the job than you do energy. Either way, you are not doing yourself or the company any good by hanging around a moment longer than necessary. Realize that this is not a critique of your talent, experience, integrity or company loyalty. You simply have gone beyond your prime and need to move on while you still can.

The first thing to do is get a medical check-up and see what is actually ailing you. If it is stress related and not permanent or terminal, do whatever you can to retire, get into a healthy lifestyle and start enjoying the rest of your life. If it is irreversible, you still owe it to yourself and your family to get the most you can out of the rest of your life. Spend time with your spouse, children, grandchildren and friends. You've worked long enough and you don't owe anything to anybody. Face it, work's killing you and if you don't do something soon, it will finish the job.

Can Level 8 happen to a younger person or one further down the chain of command? Not likely, as Level 8 symptoms only come as a last result of many failed attempts at seeking a more pleasant level or escaping the *Ten Levels* altogether. Level 8 is usually the home of an unwitting victim who had their eye focused on too firmly on Level 7 (Apathy), but ran out of the strength or will to hold that delicate balance. Younger employees will almost always fall back into a series of 3-6 Loops (Cyclic Trends) or choose to hide out in Level 2 (Nodding and Agreeing), Level 4 (Escape), one of the self-maintaining Trends.

Level 8's have gone beyond the vocational point-of-no-return need a "…it's only a job" wake-up call. Nothing is worth sacrificing your health and reducing your lifespan over. Give yourself a break; you didn't plan to end up here, it's not your fault, now move on and have some fun!

Management Perspective

As a manager of a Level 8, your goal is exactly the same as what I just told the employee. Help him/her to face reality, get healthy, and get on with the rest of their life. Level 8 is just that, a slow, unstoppable decline based on being too weak to keep fighting.

You are not being disrespectful or unfair in doing whatever it takes to help this person get the best retirement package possible and get on with planning the rest of their life. You are doing the right thing for them, their family, the company and your department. This is not a place to beat around the bush. A Level 8 will never be a capable team player. He or she may be able to offer some experienced counsel and valuable insights before they go, so use the remaining time wisely to pick their brain and let their talent and knowledge rub off on other members of your staff, but do not be fooled into thinking they will hold up under the pressure of the real world.

Chapter One

The fragile few who actually make it to Level 8 are in a place they never planned to be and, as their supervisor, the most therapeutic and caring thing you can do is help them quickly through it. Look at it this way; the faster they admit to the reality of their situation and move to make the most out of their remaining years, the better it will be for everyone.

If they are a long-term employee with political ties to the firm, be cognizant of that in working out an exit strategy, but remember: your number one goal is to make your department better, not to carry people who can't keep up. Don't be rude or hurtful, as this person is deserving of your respect for their long and dedicated service. Handle it, do what's right, then get back to reeling in your Level 3's (Griping and Complaining), 5's (Gut Check), 6's (Class Clown) and as many 4's (Escape) as you can.

Level 9 — Paranoia

Level 9 is to Level 8 (Decline and Surrender) as Level 6 (Class Clown) is to Level 5 (Gut Check) – a break from the discomfort for a while, in a warped sort of way. This is where serious mental illness (we all have casual mental illness) enters the picture and with it certain concerns as to the safety of others. Most Level 9's are either very happy or very sad, and can quickly fluctuate between the two. Their eyes wander while they are talking and they frequently forget words or subjects.

Level 9's are to the point where they actually consider alternatives for permanent escape (see Level 10). Professional help is the best you can recommend to your Level 9 friends or subordinates however don't expect them to jump at the suggestion.

Level 9 symptoms include:

- Uncontrollable laughing or sometimes even crying
- Lack of concentration
- Very low self esteem
- Willingness to jump on bandwagons

Although Level 9's may gather in Level 3 "bellyache brotherhoods" on occasion, they are not emotionally stable enough to maintain a rational conversation without either threatening someone's life or breaking down into a quivering mass. They normally travel in pairs and use each other's warped impressions of reality to justify their own.

Chapter One

...Old School Joe and Beloved Betty

Betty and Joe came from the old school. Shipping & Receiving was a small and easily managed department back then, and Betty was a wizard at coordinating incoming inspections and scheduling product shipments to a growing number of locations. When she started back in 1974, it was a manual task, using handwritten charts and large, wall-sized calendars to plan shipping deadlines and materials receipts. As the size of the department, the complexity of the operations, and the use of computer technology grew, Betty began to experience more stress and pressure with her expanding job responsibilities. Like most of her counterparts, she could sometimes be found participating in Level 3 "fret frats" during breaks and at lunchtime. It was a harmless way of purging some of the day's frustration and actually became kind of fun, reeling in an occasional Level 6 (Class Clown) or two.

Like many regularly enjoyed pastimes, however, whining and moaning soon began to be a habit for Betty. She didn't realize that it was slowly undermining her normally positive attitude. What was a simple form of ventilation therapy that posed no real harm was now becoming a part of her personality below her conscious awareness. It wasn't going unnoticed by others in her department, however.

Joe and Betty became friends through their involvement in the lunchtime ritual of venting their unhappiness about various aspects of their work. Joe was the foreman over the Tool Crib and could match every one of Betty's shipping nightmares with a similar experience transpiring around some lost or broken piece of tooling or missing grinding wheel. As with negative habit patterns that revolve around the "…you're not going to believe this one…" type of stories, the two started to feed off each other. They began to take their casual membership in various "carp clusters" to new heights of proficiency that they found gratifying. Others soon began to distance themselves from this group, though, as it became more serious and less just simple fun.

Before long, Betty and Joe were actually getting more power and exhilaration from their shared paranoia during story times than from their actual jobs. This phenomenon allowed them to continue to perform their jobs proficiently, while avoiding most of the Level 4 (Escape), 5 (Gut Check) and 6 (Class Clown) symptoms that many of their peers were experiencing.

There is certainly nothing wrong with missing out on several of the most debilitating levels during your career. Unfortunately, Level 9 becomes a box canyon, much like

Level 2 (Nodding and Agreeing) or Level 4 (Escape). It provides a rush and some strength to carry on, but becomes its own self-maintaining trend. After years of practice, the advanced Level 9 becomes skilled at "making mountains out of mole hills" and develops a paranoid fear and an overly emotional view of everything that is going on. Level 9's need the fix of dwelling on and expanding the influence of events and experiences during their work day, very much like the Level 4 needs that one more beer at last call.

Because they began this habit pattern as a positive way to alleviate growing frustration, and initially it worked, most Level 9's do not see the subtle changes in their motives until they are finally pointed out by a concerned coworker. Only the most well-meaning friends will even offer this advice, and when they do, it will usually be met by immediate denial and defensiveness, much like the alcoholic defends his or her "social drinking."

Level 9's can be very destructive to an organization, because they are often people who were initially respected by a wide range of other employees. Since they feed on each other and develop an emotional need for the stimulus of the game, their numbers can grow geometrically, once they get a foothold. It is very easy for other employees with frustrations on their minds to be absorbed into these negative groups, which lowers the morale of a widening circle of influence.

It takes a long time for Level 9 status to reach a dangerous stage, so management should be on the lookout and attempt to catch and neutralize these behaviors early. The only solution for a serious, terminal case may be too strongly suggest exercising an early retirement option or intimating an unfavorable transfer.

Employee Perspective

Every company has a small number of Level 9's floating around, but I doubt if many will be reading this book. If you're one, congratulations, you are already on the right track. Level 9 is where you end up if you survive or sneak around Level 8 (Decline and Surrender) and don't take the advice in the last chapter. Others of you simply skipped a bunch of levels, avoided getting in the "Cyclic Trends" or the other "Self-Maintaining Trends" and got here when the habit of negativity became your reason for living.

Good news, it's all in your head! I don't mean to make fun of the situation, but it's true. You are a "glass is half empty" person to the extreme. You need to either "get over it", get back to a more positive outlook and rejoin the functional members of your department, or get the professional help you need to do it. There is nothing wrong with admitting to some mental challenges and getting the assistance of a good shrink to get you back to a productive and happy life.

I can guarantee you that one of the first steps will be to change who you spend time with. Level 9's pair up and cry on each other's shoulder, so you need to break away or get your Level 9 friend(s) to get healed with you; not too likely. Definitely try it, but don't expect the members of your favorite "gripe group" to gleefully jump at the chance to go get their head shrunk with you. If it were that easy, you'd all have done it already. This is a decision about you and it's your time to get it right. You have no idea how much you're missing with that dark cloud over your head all the time.

Management Perspective

Level 9 is a rather diverse group, so you need to do a little homework before dealing with them. While they are not hard to identify using the above symptoms, depending on their age, sex, job level, and the others in their favorite "pout posse", you will find that there is no one right way to deal with them. The one universal truth is that they do not realize how much time and effort they put into "woe is me" – time that is being taken away from their job, and you're paying for it!

The best initial test question may be just that; confront them with the truth, that they are wasting time on the company's dime, and see their reaction. If it gets them thinking, feeling a bit embarrassed, or apologetic, you might have a chance. If they get defensive and angry, you have a case where they will need help beyond what you are qualified to give.

Once again, these folks are not going to be easily won back to the team, and during a time when you have good potential with your more malleable staffers, you can't afford to spend too much time guessing. If the person in question is a younger employee, they are worth some initial effort, assuming you get reaction #1, above. If they are older and set in their ways you should either leave them alone, as long as they are not bringing down the whole department, or get assistance from upper management.

You do not want to fight with Level 9's, anger them, or make them into a bigger problem than they already are. Usually, low self esteem is a prerequisite for Level 9 issues, and that is something that you can do only so much to build up. Self esteem issues come from a very young age, as early as 4-6 years old, and are the result of poor parenting or negative involvement with other authority figures. Much of their issues are deeply subconscious and may require professional help, something well beyond the scope of a caring supervisor or friend.

My suggestion is to make a rapid diagnosis, then get the help you need to keep your Level 9's from infecting the rest of your people. This kind of negative, gossipy behavior is very contagious and can undermine a broad range of people quickly. Level 9's are to be separated, then dealt with as quickly as possible.

Level 10 — Insanity

The final level is pretty self-explanatory. When all other attempts have been exhausted, an individual will succumb to "Workplace Insanity." Psychologists tell us we all have a pre-chosen escape route in our subconscious mind should we ever need it, so this level is an automatic final step, when all else fails.

There are no symptoms of Level 10, because by the time someone chooses this level, it is too late to diagnose. Hopefully, a Level 10 will not harm themselves or others in carrying out their decision, but this is an area in which much is theorized, but nothing is consistent enough to anticipate. Only a very small percentage of our nation's employee base ever approaches Level 10, and an even smaller percentage actually follows through. While that is reassuring, it is still well advised to have some understanding of the subtle characteristics that may lead to this level.

...this is
"Love-my-job"
Earl

Chapter One

Earl was one of those guys whose whole life revolved around his work. Everyone knew that he would never retire, but hoped he would find some other interests outside the office. Ever since that nasty divorce back in 2002, he has buried himself in his work to overcome the pain and loneliness. He doesn't seem sad or lonely, and his work of negotiating large projects for the Corporate Special Projects department is unparalleled in the company. Earl is a pillar of the community and a positive spokesman for the company in social settings and in dealings with both customers and vendors. This is the last guy who people would wonder about, unless they really got to know him.

Earl's ability to hold his emotions well in check has made it difficult to categorize him in the *Ten Levels of Workplace Disillusionment* for any length of time. When things get tough, he seems to be able to take a deep breath and move on unabashed. While this certainly has been beneficial in his ability to work well with others and achieve multiple promotions during his 26-year career, the internal effects went unnoticed for a long time. When they finally reared their ugly head, Earl's symptoms were vague and inconsistent. Bouts of forgetfulness, periods of quiet "insanity" where he seemed to be in another world, uncharacteristic anger at what were normally "no big deal" issues for him. His peers and subordinates at first just shrugged these episodes off under the heading of "everybody has a bad day now and then."

Because of his internal focus, and ability to keep problems bottled up inside, he never outwardly demonstrated any of the common Level 3 (Griping and Complaining), Level 5 (Gut Check), or Level 8 (Decline & Surrender) symptoms of frustration or resentment that many of the other employees experienced as they climbed the corporate ladder. He probably did go through these levels, but was able to masterfully hide them from those around who had too many of their own problems to deal with to question the unshared issues of Earl who always appeared to have it all together.

When they finally came and hauled Earl off, it was a shock to everybody in his department. All of life's pressures finally added up and overcame Earl's ability to hold them at bay. Fortunately, Earl did not do damage to himself or others, but in other Level 10 situations it could have been drastically different. A very small percentage of the American workforce experiences Level 10, so it is difficult for management to either anticipate or react to warning signs. Obviously, the Type A workaholic, with minimal outside interests, is a possible indication. However, it is really nobody's business what employees do with their personal time, so it is not always easy to determine when, or if, to step in.

Because of its very limited application and indistinguishable symptoms, Level 10 is one of those unavoidable statistics that will plague many companies from time to time. Management's goal (hopefully) of identifying negative behavior patterns, confronting them in cooperation with the employee, and implementing new options for a healthier work experience may serve to catch potential Level 10 candidates long before they reach a point where Level 10 is a viable life option.

Employee Perspective

If you were actually a Level 10 you would not be reading this book, so I'm going to talk to you as if you were not yet there, just kicking the tires. Don't do it, man! You are either a Level 8 (Decline & Surrender), or Level 9 (Paranoia), so the first thing to do is go back and reread the last two chapters. My advice to you would be similar to a Level 8, get life in perspective. If your job is really making you nuts, it isn't worth it. Get some help, train for a marathon, change your hobbies, make a change.

Level 10 is a very rare level and the folks who get here usually do it fast and without warning. Some do damage to themselves, sometimes to others, and in some cases both. Either way you don't come back from it, so don't take the chance. You're not a Level 10, now go get the help you need!

Management Perspective

Good news; you may never have to deal with a Level 10 during your entire career. Better news; if you do, it will be something you have no warning about, or control over, so you won't be at fault. Bad news; it's never pretty. "Workplace Insanity" is just that – insane, so you can't anticipate it, fix it, understand it or correct it. It's some kind of a meltdown, and there's rarely a ready disaster plan. Fallout can include a gap in your team and a domino effect of "down time." Your job is to protect the rest of your people from it. It is rare and over fast, so I wouldn't worry too much about Level 10 readiness.

THE TEN LEVELS

1—*DISBELIEF*

2—*NODDING & AGREEING*

3—*GRIPING & COMPLAINING*

4—*ESCAPE*

5—*GUT CHECK*

6—*CLASS CLOWN*

7—*APATHY*

8—*DECLINE & SURRENDER*

9—*PARANOIA*

10—*INSANITY*

Chapter One •

Summation

    The majority of employees who enter the *Ten Levels* slip relatively quickly through Level 1 (Disbelief) and Level 2 (Nodding and Agreeing). Fortunately, not very many travel through Levels 8 (Decline and Surrender), 9 (Paranoia) and 10 (Insanity) during their career. Most of those who remain stuck within the *Ten Levels* get out at or before Level 8 through retirement, disability, or premature death.

    The majority of us bounce around between Level 3 (Griping and Complaining) and Level 6 (Class Clown). The next largest group hides out in Level 4 (Escape), with a smaller percentage settling for Level 2 (Nodding and Agreeing) and Level 9 (Paranoia). A few are able to balance on Level 7 (Apathy), until they retire. The lucky ones get out of the game altogether and take on a whole other array of challenges by either working in a more motivating, less political job, or by starting their own businesses.

    It has taken 20 years of tinkering and fine tuning to get the *Ten Levels* to where they are today. They are now the definitive building blocks of workplace dysfunction and, in that sense, provide a track to run on in evaluating the morale, productivity, performance, teamwork and hidden potential of any workplace, in any industry. Each level is an exercise in realizing and understanding the power of habit and how it hooks people out of desperation, discomfort or convenience into ways of handling the day to day stress of work.

    Over the years, I've been amazed at the way different personality types tended to follow each other like lemmings into the same cycles or traps, often wasting vast portions of their working life. After more intensely observing and researching from the sidelines for the last few years, it was time to jump back in with some observations, suggestions and a helpful tool to get everybody to look honestly at their way of living at work and together pulling each other out of the quicksand.

While we have spent a lot of time delving into the *Ten Levels*, this is really a four-part approach with the ultimate goal of helping everyone out of the prison that a work life within the levels represents. Chapter One introduces the premise behind the study of the *Ten Levels*. This part is like basic math – you get each principle one at a time and need to develop a proficiency in working with them before you are ready to use them in equations.

Chapter Two is the Algebra; viewing the levels as they react and intertwine with each other like recurring equations of life. This is where you will get a true feel for where you stand and, hopefully, gain confidence to help you and your coworkers get out of the cycle.

Chapter Three is the Calculus, where the rubber meets the road; the real-world applications that make studying the fundamentals pay off. Getting off of the Merry-Go-Round is what this book is all about. Fortunately, I have done it and have some great tools to share that can help you and your fellow employees do it too.

Employee Perspective

I studied the *Ten Levels* from the inside during my early years in the corporate workforce, then for 15 more years from the other side, as a recognition consultant to the managerial side, so I have had the benefit of molding my views about the levels from multiple perspectives over a long period of time. The next chapter is the meat and potatoes of this book, so I strongly suggest you get yourself as familiar as possible with the *Ten Levels*, and get a feel for them. It will make it easier to appreciate the subtleties of the Trends in the next two chapters.

A good working knowledge of the *Ten Levels* will also

Chapter One

help you in dealing with your coworkers. You will have the advantage of paying attention to the behaviors, the dialogue, and the reactions of other people as they interact, rather than missing portions while you strive to remember which level symptoms they are exhibiting.

Hey, it's only Ten – memorize it! Just humor me for now! You'll thank me after Chapter 3.

THE TEN LEVELS

1—*DISBELIEF*

2—*NODDING & AGREEING*

3—*GRIPING & COMPLAINING*

4—*ESCAPE*

5—*GUT CHECK*

6—*CLASS CLOWN*

7—*APATHY*

8—*DECLINE & SURRENDER*

9—*PARANOIA*

10—*INSANITY*

Management Perspective

Instructing your employees on the dynamics of the *Ten Levels of Workplace Disillusionment* can result in a happier, more productive staff. Your thorough knowledge of the *Ten Levels* and the Trends will make this process more rewarding, because you may find that you exhibit some of these reactionary tendencies and must deal with them before you can lead your team in overcoming theirs.

As a trainer, motivator and coach to your employees, the knowledge you both have of the *Ten Levels* will give you some excellent tools to use in working to improve all aspects of workplace activity. I may be a little bit biased towards my version of why people do what they do at work, but in reality any tool that gets you and your workers singing from the same hymn book, will give you the opportunity to generate fresh enthusiasm for the many ways whereby work can be more enjoyable and productive for all of you.

There is, however, a risk in helping your employees confront and deal with the causes or negative behavior patterns that affect them – you may be giving them the inner strength and confidence they need to leave your firm and go on to other greener pastures! While there is no denying the potential of this happening, the benefits if they stay are the seeds of a better working environment that will sprout up and intertwine with all your other employees now and in the future. In the same vein as tuition reimbursement and other work-related training, the improvements in the people you keep will far outweigh the loss of the ones who inevitably leave.

Get More Productivity for Less Money . . . Your Employees will Love You for It

Chapter 2
Some Common Trends

Although everyone has a favorite level where they find comfort or justification for their discomfort, nobody stays in any one level all of the time. Some of your wimpiest Level 2's (Nodding and Agreeing), the most strung-out Level 4's (Escape), and the most resolute Level 9's (Paranoia) appear to be stuck there, but they all started out at Level 1 (Disbelief) and can get coaxed into other levels from time to time, even though they may hide it from the rest of us. Interaction with other people and job related or personal challenges also work to alter our levels regularly. Close scrutiny has distinguished some trends in the way many of us slide up and down the chart.

Two types of trends exist throughout the *Ten Levels of Workplace Disillusionment*. I call them Cyclic Trends and Self-Maintaining Trends.

Cyclic Trends

> 1—DISBELIEF 2—NODDING & AGREEING
> 3—GRIPING & COMPLAINING 4—ESCAPE
> 5—GUT CHECK 6—CLASS CLOWN 7—APATHY
> 8—SURRENDER 9—PARANOIA 10—INSANITY

The 3-6 Loop

The 3-6 Loop is the most noteworthy cyclic trend besetting professionals in project-oriented positions. I was a big time "3-6 Looper" as an Industrial Engineer in my first two jobs after college. The jump from Level 1 (Disbelief) to 2 (Nodding and Agreeing), for most new employees, is quite rapid. The jump from Level 2 to Level 3 (Griping and Complaining) is even faster. This represents the "look out world, here I come" attitude that many college grads bring to their first jobs, because they have a lot of knowledge, ego and naivety, but no understanding of corporate politics.

Due to the stress and confusion associated with residing

Chapter Two •

in Level 3 and constantly trying to find a valuable contribution to make, Level 4 (Escape) and Level 5 (Gut Check) inevitably become considerations. The self motivated achiever will normally not be lured into Level 4, at least the first few times around the loop. Level 5 (Gut Check), however, is ready and waiting for the "go-getter" who enthusiastically bounds over Level 4 (Escape) toward success.

The tricky part of Level 5 (Gut Check) is that it creeps up subtly and isn't noticeable to others. Add to that the fact that it often affects younger employees who feel invincible at this stage of life and may be putting in some long, dedicated hours at the expense of proper diet and exercise, which results in a person ripe for internal complications. The struggling achiever seems to be functioning normally while he or she is actually experiencing unfamiliar internal annoyances.

1—DISBELIEF
2—NODDING & AGREEING
3—GRIPING & COMPLAINING
4—ESCAPE
5—GUT CHECK
6—CLASS CLOWN
7—APATHY
8—SURRENDER
9—PARANOIA
10—INSANITY

I don't know about you, but I have found intestinal pain to be very difficult to endure for a long period of time. This tends to explain the transference to Level 6 (Class Clown) for a reprieve. It also can lead to some explanation of why a perfectly normal, hardworking employee can suddenly fall into Level 4 after a few laps around the 3-6 Loop. Level 6 inhabitants are very congenial and light hearted. I venture to say that many of your offices "good time Charlies" are

Level 6 aficionados. Although borderline loony, the Level 6 sojourner is often just taking a breather from his fast-paced success plan to have some fun. The longer an individual fights to stay out of Level 5, the more likely they are to experience the more severe peculiarities of Level 6, then he or she finally succumbs to goofing off. Sometimes, though, the medications taken to survive prolonged stays in Level 5, or the innocent couple of beers after work, can slowly begin to make our valuable contributor a candidate for Level 4 rather than Level 6 the next time around the loop. What makes it so dangerous is that, like Level 5, Level 4 is not a planned escape for the high achiever. It just starts to develop into a habit pattern of socially acceptable stress relief and then escalates from there.

Level 7 (Apathy) is an island. It is a turning point incomprehensible to the young achiever, because apathy at this stage in his or her career is not an option. Visualizing Level 7 only creates anger and aggravation, because it is like quitting. So where do you go after mellowing out in Level 6 (Class Clown) for a while? There are three options:

- Back to Level 3 (Griping and Complaining), when the next fresh challenge comes your way, to begin another trip around the 3-6 Loop.

- On to Level 7 (Apathy), for the attempt to maintain a noncommittal position towards work, until retirement, without experiencing significant guilt feelings.

- Break free from the cycle by joining with a group of fellow employees who support each other and have common goals, or by starting your own business outside the restrictions of corporate politics.

Frankly, the third, and most obvious, choice is usually not selected. This is due to fear and ego conflicts we all possess, and because tools like *The Vocational Shrink's Communications Training Program* have not been available to offer a believable alternative. Many of our country's best run companies are beginning to make option three groups available to their employees to avoid losing them to the system, independent business opportunities, or competitors that concentrate more on employee fulfillment programs.

I didn't have these options when I got out of school, so I ran the 3-6 Loop a bunch of times, learned all about self employment the hard way, and finally wrote this book. One of my goals is to save some people from traveling the whole, lonely path to fulfillment by themselves, as so many before them have tried to do. We can only guess how many people who stayed in the system until it was too late could have been helped if this book had been around sooner. I plan to make up for all those lost souls, by helping everyone I can now.

Better yet, perhaps I can have some impact on helping supervisors improve the quality of the workplace. When both employees and their managers are cognizant of and have a desire to improve the situation, the need to hole up in negative behavior levels and trends diminishes.

Even with change beginning to happen in the understanding of employee recognition, motivation, and fulfillment, the plight of many of our society's young, aggressive achievers is to run the 3-6 Loop over and over until they finally exit through the ever present temptation of Level 4 (Escape), the self defeatist attitude of Level 9 (Paranoia), or the elusive nirvana of Level 7 (Apathy).

The Fulcrum – Level 7

```
1—DISBELIEF  2—NODDING &
AGREEING  3—GRIPING &
COMPLAINING  4—ESCAPE
5—GUT CHECK  6—CLASS CLOWN
7—APATHY  8—SURRENDER
9—PARANOIA  10—INSANITY
```

The notable break in the *Ten Levels of Workplace Disillusionment* falls between Level 6 (Class Clown) and Level 7 (Apathy). There are a lot of "pseudo 7's" around, but the trained eye can discern them as "3-6 Loopers" experiencing another Level 6 delusion of grandeur. True Level 7's have made the choice to stay where they are forever (or at least until pending retirement). They don't want to

• **Some Common Trends**

make any waves or upset their routine, "...just leave me alone, I retire in 4 years, 3 months, 6 days, and 3 ½ hours." The problem with most Level 7's is that they were in the 3-6 Loop for years and the idea of just jumping off at the top of the pendulum, so to speak, is very foreign to their character and lifelong habits. They are fed up with the 3-6 Loop, but scared to death of dropping over the top into Levels 8, 9, or 10. The longer they wait to take on the Fulcrum, though, the less chance they will have to balance it effectively. It is a "Catch 22" between conserving enough energy to maintain a balance on the Fulcrum, and waiting until they are close enough to retirement to kick into their final sprint. This need for such precise timing is why it is so difficult to pull off a true Level 7 experience.

When someone who is used to being frustrated and challenged every day decides to try something different, but realizes they are too old and out of vocational shape to change careers, the immediate sensation is one of relief. The long-term result, however, may be a slow slide into self-pity, and a realization of old age setting in. By definition, apathy assumes you are of no real value other than in your high level of skill at ducking at all the right times and avoiding any kind of responsibility...hello, Level 8 (Decline and Surrender)!

Unfortunately, once Level 8 symptoms begin to appear there is usually no turning back. The body and mind begin the slow process of degeneration, often followed by retirement and an early demise. That's why even the few apparent Level 7 (Apathy) success stories don't often end up in successful, energetic, long lasting retirement experiences. The habit is simply too hard to break, and any Level 8 symptoms that did begin only make it harder.

Well, so much for the oasis of Level 7. Staying on the Fulcrum as the pendulum swings back to Level 3 (Griping and Complaining), and over to Level 8 is extremely difficult and taxing on the system (sounds a little like Level 3, again, doesn't it?). The only way I've seen someone remain in Level 7 is to keep so actively involved in outside activities that they can put in their hours at work and not get into the internal politics. It translates into bringing the body to work and leaving the mind at home, and that is the ultimate waste for both the company and the employee.

Self-Maintaining Trends

1—DISBELIEF 2—NODDING & AGREEING 3—GRIPING & COMPLAINING 4—ESCAPE
5—GUT CHECK 6—CLASS CLOWN 7—APATHY 8—SURRENDER 9—PARANOIA 10—INSANITY

The Trap – Level 2

People who dwell in Level 2 (Nodding and Agreeing) for very long are candidates for the Trap. Individuals with low self-esteem, inadequate or outdated skills and limited drive can easily find ways to justify permanent residence in Level 2. Fear and lack of self respect, combined with "Peter Principle" (Level 2 – Nodding and Agreeing) incompetence, is the recipe for the Trap. Although most of us would be uncomfortable "sucking up" all the time, the knowledge that we are in a position and a salary range far greater than we could achieve anywhere else creates a comfort zone, in a warped sense of the word.

"Trappers" can be very bad for a company, because they will agree with the boss no matter what he or she says. At best, this affords no creative input or help to the company's leaders. At worst, it can give the boss a false sense of capability that may lead to costly mistakes in judgment, and inefficient utilization of company resources.

It is poor stewardship on the company's part to allow employees to flounder aimlessly on the payroll. If the boss believes that he can do everything himself, without the help of real experts (his Level 2 "experts" are a sham), the company suffers and is at risk of being overtaken by better-managed competition.

There is a lot of guilt associated with Level 2, either by the employee who misuses his or her position or by the employer who allows it to happen, or both. In the situations I have witnessed, the worst Level 2's are there as a favor to pay a past business debt and are simply too selfish to bow out gracefully and rejoin the functional world. They are content to carry a prestigious title, rake in the paycheck, the benefits and the perks. These people are few, in this day and age, but astute management and common sense go a long way toward recognizing and eradicating the company of this negative situation. Level 2's are quickly identified and eliminated in a family business when competent, professional management is brought in and the "good ol' boy" network loses power. Unfortunately, this often takes the death of the founding entrepreneur who would never seek retirement and cannot be easily forced out.

The Escape – Level 4

Escape from the struggles of day-to-day life (drugs, alcohol, gambling and other addictions), is common practice for many people. The problem, as with most habits, occurs when socially acceptable, voluntary escape becomes a necessary activity no longer controllable by the user. The option to move from the stresses of Level

3 (Griping and Complaining) to the perceived contentment of Level 4 (Escape) can be pretty tough to resist, making it the easiest out available for many. Add to that how easy it is for that innocent couple of beers after work to become a needed fix, or those few pills taken from time to time (usually for hidden Level 5 symptoms) to become a daily ritual, and you can see why bars and casinos are so busy.

The Escape victim is the person who lacks the self-discipline and peer support to use chemicals in moderation or not at all. As in the Trap, he or she finds ways to justify remaining in an unhealthy state. The rationale is based on a subconscious dependence on the drugs (they could never consciously admit to an addiction) rather than on fear and incompetence, as with Level 2 (Nodding and Agreeing). A lack of self-confidence and its associated anxiety can contribute to a person's involvement in the Escape, but the continued use of chemicals to relieve frustration affects the mind's ability to generate rational thought patterns – and rational thought patterns are the only way out. Level 4 is characterized by a worsening spiral, a true self-destructive, self-maintaining trend.

The Whiner – Level 9

What starts out as innocent banter about the daily frustrations of the workday can ultimately lead to an almost addictive need for a regular dose of complaining. Level 3's (Griping and Complaining) sometimes get so into the antics of their favorite "remonstration organization" that it becomes their drug of choice. When this happens, they will team up with another one or two people with a similar weakness and literally feed off of each other's negativism. While this goes unnoticed within the group, they start to be seen as chronic complainers, and that really turns off those "glass is half full" producers that you value so much in your organization.

It is important for management to identify, isolate and individually work with these people to wean them from this habit. If it is caught and brought to their attention early enough, Whiners may be receptive to the corrective criticism and realize that they have gotten a little carried away with the extent and vociferousness of their impatience with company systems and procedures. You may be able to make them a part of the solution, rather than allowing them to remain a part of the problem, and bring them back to a position where they are productive and positive again. They may still be prime candidates for normal Level 3 behavior, but hopefully will be cognizant of the point where healthy discussions begin to turn into overreactions, and will know when to quit.

If you get to them too late for a healthy turnaround, you are left to deal with them as you would a Level 2 (Nodding and Agreeing) or Level 4 (Escape). They need to be led to a realistic and low-visibility retirement or resignation option. The goal is to allow them to save face, without getting into a battle of wits that can never be won, and which only serves to substantiate what everyone already knows.

Hints to Identifying Levels

1—DISBELIEF 2—NODDING & AGREEING 3—GRIPING & COMPLAINING 4—ESCAPE
5—GUT CHECK 6—CLASS CLOWN 7—APATHY 8—SURRENDER 9—PARANOIA 10—INSANITY

As an employee or supervisor, one of the greatest initial challenges of using the information in *The Vocational Shrink's Communications Training Program* will be identifying levels. When implementing the program into your workplace, the ability to quickly and accurately identify the various levels you and your fellow workers are using on a day-to-day basis is the key to progress and a continued effort by all parties.

One of the best ways to do this is to ask a question. Depending on the answer, you will often be able to quickly identify their current level and begin to work through the process of determining the personality characteristics, habit patterns and stimuli that are causing the negative reaction. Remember, for this to work it needs to be honest, empathetic, fun, and non-threatening. Only revelations thoroughly embraced by an employee have any hope of being acted upon. Here are a few examples:

1. Ask a committing question such as:
   "How do you think we ought to do such and such?"

   A **Level 1** will – sigh, roll their eyes or look upwards, and deliberate over the response that will make them look most like a team player.

   A **Level 2** will – talk around the question and try to change the subject to a non-business related area. Or, he might become angry and refuse to respond, using some excuse as to the validity of the question based on your job description.

   A **Level 3** will – offer two or three solutions and volunteer to spearhead the project.

   A **Level 4** will – probably misunderstand the question or attempt to show why it doesn't involve him or her.

   A **Level 5** will – smile, wince, excuse him or herself, and hurry off towards the facilities. Or, they'll respond much like a Level 3, then smile, wince, excuse themselves and hurry off towards the facilities.

   A **Level 6** will – be reminded of a joke.

   A **Level 7** will – chuckle, and then slowly respond with a blue sky solution that would never fly within the existing budget structure.

   [Don't ask questions of Level 8's, 9's and 10's!]

1—DISBELIEF **2**—NODDING & AGREEING **3**—GRIPING & COMPLAINING **4**—ESCAPE
5—GUT CHECK **6**—CLASS CLOWN **7**—APATHY **8**—SURRENDER **9**—PARANOIA **10**—INSANITY

2. Compliment the person in a personal, non-performance related area such as:
   "That's a sharp looking new car, Joyce."

   A **Level 1** will – smile big, thank you a little more than you feel the compliment is due, and try to make friends. He or she will probably ask a company policy-related question, if you react positively to their gesture.

   A **Level 2** will – deny the validity of the gesture and wonder what you want them to do (a step backwards, wringing of hands, and/or a nervous grin may accompany the comment).

   A **Level 3** will – tell you the complete history of the particular model and manufacturer and then expound on how to get a good deal on one.

   A **Level 4** will – probably misunderstand the comment or attempt to show why it doesn't involve them.

   A **Level 5** will – thank you graciously, then smile, wince, excuse themselves and hurry off towards the facilities.

   A **Level 6** will – laugh, make a joke about the car, and then break into an impression of a coworker stuck in traffic.

   A **Level 7** will – be taken aback at the idea that someone would extend a positive observation their way, then slowly recount the story of their first car and how fun it was to drive it in the country with the top down.

3. Ask a question about personal goals like:
   "Where do you see yourself in three years, Bruce?"

   A **Level 1** will – sigh, seriously consider the question, and then respond with a canned answer they think you want to hear.

   A **Level 2** will – feel threatened, beat around the bush, avoid the question, become uncomfortable about his or her privacy being invaded (they know they'll be doing exactly the same thing in three years, barring a major upper management change).

1—DISBELIEF **2**—NODDING & AGREEING **3**—GRIPING & COMPLAINING **4**—ESCAPE
5—GUT CHECK **6**—CLASS CLOWN **7**—APATHY **8**—SURRENDER **9**—PARANOIA **10**—INSANITY

A **Level 3** will – mention several "fast lane" ideas and describe the people, places, and specific short- and long-term goals involved in the plan.

A **Level 4** will—probably misunderstand the question or attempt to show why it doesn't involve him or her.

A **Level 5** will – get initially enthusiastic about goals and dreams, then smile, wince, excuse themselves and hurry off towards the facilities.

A **Level 6** will – laugh, say something strange like "a tightrope walker with Barnum and Bailey", then begin humming the circus theme like a calliope.

A **Level 7** will – chuckle, and go into excruciating detail about his hideaway in the mountains with the babbling brook, and the animals, and the peace, and the serenity…

These are just a few examples, but they demonstrate how easy it is to design questions relevant to your business and workforce that will quickly identify and categorize your people in a simple and non-confrontive manner.

Summation

Understanding the way the *Ten Levels* fit into trends is helpful in predicting how different personality types will vacillate between levels during their work lives. As trends develop, the habits that control the choices which lead to reactive options become grouped in a repeatable series. Elimination of the control and time lost to the *Ten Levels* becomes more and more difficult as people unknowingly fall into the clutches of various behavioral trends.

The problem is rooted in the very way our minds are built to work. The subconscious mind always provides what it thinks we want out of life based on all the information we've put in since we were born. Most of our decisions every day are subconsciously generated from deep-seated beliefs stored in the subconscious, so they occur without thought or question. The first step in changing behavior is the awareness of our habits, and then using our current levels of information and logic to reconsider the actions.

One of my favorite Star Trek episodes, "Shore Leave" (Season 1, Episode 15 for you Trekies) is the one where the crew of the Enterprise lands on a recreational planet for some R&R. Captain Kirk ends up meeting a rival from his academy days and they fight just like old times while Mr. Sulu is attacked by a Samurai Warrior and must fight to the death. Each crew member confronts one of their hidden demons that was locked up deep in their mind, until the advanced race that runs the planet realizes that the primitive Earth people are not mentally sophisticated enough to use his planet as it was designed.

This recreational facility allows each guest to create any experience in their mind to enjoy as if it were real. Unfortunately, these lowly humans allowed negative thoughts to enter their heads and the planet, much like our own subconscious mind, simply created these realities, without questioning whether or not they were right. Sadly, many people go through their whole lives allowing negative, scary, self-limiting thoughts to control their mind, and their subconscious dutifully makes sure that their desires are found in the world around them.

This is the most profound and powerful revelation I can share with you, and it's a major key to why some people are far more successful, capable and happy than other people. It's not brains, talent, or luck that makes the difference, but what we believe and expect from ourselves that determines how far we can go. The use of *The Vocational Shrink's Communications Training Program* in an unintimidating and supportive atmosphere could lead to a healthy realization of time spent in various levels and trends. This simple act of bringing subconscious behavior patterns into the conscious mind will provide an opportunity to consider how new habits can forge a far happier, healthier and profitable work environment.

Get More Productivity for Less Money . . . Your Employees will Love You for It

Chapter 3
Using the Ten Levels to Make Changes

For all of you who read the last page of a book first, peek at the results of the Motor Trend new car comparisons before reading the article, or just plain visualize a short cut in everything—surprise! The previous two chapters represent the first step to getting off the merry-go-round. So if you haven't read them yet, nice try. Go back to the beginning!

How to Get Off the Merry-go-round

Believe it or not, this part is simple (not easy, but simple – like baseball!) Actually, getting off the merry-go-round is a lot easier than the games we all go through scampering up and down the *Ten Levels* year after year. There are three steps to counteracting a life of habitual frustration living within the *Ten Levels of Workplace Disillusionment*, or to changing any habit for that matter. Before looking at the steps to changing habits, let's discuss how habits are developed and how dominating they are to our lives.

Habits are reactions that we choose, without conscious thought, based on programming that has been entered into our subconscious minds throughout our lives. The human subconscious mind works similar to a computer. It takes in stimulus and outputs what it thinks we want based on the beliefs that we have stored in our memory banks. It does this automatically, all the time.

Our subconscious does not distinguish between positive and negative input, it simply gives us what the input appears to represent based on this extensive library of beliefs, fears and predetermined responses. Each of our libraries includes all the things that have happened to us and been told to us by parents, teachers, friends, heroes

– anyone seen as an authority figure – not necessarily an authority figure now, but when the experience happened to us! A person may have been an authority figure when we were young because we feared them, not because they were smart or right. Perhaps older children had a profound influence on us, including bullies and con artists. A belief does not have to be valid to control our future decision-making, only believed. That is why it is important to evaluate all questionable past beliefs from a current, adult perspective and decide if they are valuable to our life today.

Here's an example. Remember the last time you were with a group and saw a snake or lizard? Some people may have wanted to touch or hold it, while others ran for cover. The same stimulus yields completely different, totally subconscious reactions in that instant, affecting each person without thought. They probably didn't calmly whip out their trusty trail guide to identify the species and determine if it was poisonous, then decide if it was safe to approach. No, most people have a preprogrammed reaction to reptiles that elicits an immediate reaction based on some earlier (perhaps much earlier) situation, and that decision has never since been questioned.

According to Brian Tracy in his critically acclaimed *Psychology of Achievement*, more than 90 percent of the things we do each day are controlled by this same kind of response, based entirely on feelings, fears, beliefs – ultimately decisions, made and stored throughout our early life, most of them by the time we were five or six years old. Think about that for a minute. Almost every response we have to what goes on around us is controlled subconsciously by habits that were formed from events affecting us made as a young child.

The first step to all self-improvement is self-evaluation of our beliefs and the habits we've formed based on those beliefs. That means we must begin to think about the reactions we have to every stimulus that comes our way and consciously determine if the reaction we have, or the action we take, is the one we really want. Is it still valid today, considering what I know to be true? Is it moving me ahead or holding me back? Is it a well-thought-out, realistic response, or a habitual reaction based on old information that is not best for my life today? If you are like me, this process will be surprising, and quite embarrassing in many cases. But until we begin to identify and question our habitual reactions to life, we will be limited in seeing how our movement within the *Ten Levels* can be interpreted.

While I'd suggest that our objective should be to become aware of our habit patterns, in general, it's common that people prefer to stay with problems they understand, rather than look for solutions that make them uncomfortable. It is also true, however, that people do not really decide their future, they decide their habits. And then their habits decide their future . . .

Now that you have a real interest and a burning desire to evaluate and modify some reactionary behaviors, let's look at the three steps to changing any habit: awareness, support and practice.

Awareness

Ever notice how when we tell someone something about themselves they will tend to doubt or justify it, but if it's an idea they think of, it's true? Until you bring your actions into your conscious mind for evaluation based on your current knowledge and experience, it's doubtful you will ever change a behavior. You have to do this yourself. Any life change requires a personal desire to change. The reason you don't have that desire now is because the current habit is authorized by a subconscious belief that is never questioned. Once you bring it out on the table and look at it through today's eyes, you will see that – while it was an appropriate response at some time in your life – it may not be the best choice any longer.

Chapter Three •

Transactional Analysis is a theory that defines three areas of the human mind: The Parent, The Adult and The Child. The Parent is the part of the brain that holds all of the rules and regulations that you received from parents, teachers and other authority figures during your upbringing.

Some are positive, some negative, and some outdated "old wives' tales", but they're rooted there for subconscious retrieval nonetheless. "You are the spitting image of your father," "You're never going to be as smart as your sister," "Don't run with a sharp object," etc. This part of your brain acts as the parent or guardian of your mind. The Nurturing Parent is the loving, caring, supportive side. The Critical Parent holds all the do's and don'ts.

The Child area of the mind is made up of the Rebellious Child (the prankster, risk taker, rebel) and the Spontaneous Child (the playful, fun-loving, dancing, singing, crazy, carefree, careless, lazy part of your brain). This portion of your personality never grows up; it has no willpower, no self control and no discipline. That's where your fun and wild side lives.

The Adult side is the logical, conscious, "here and now" part of your brain. It is able to think things through and make logical determinations, based on all of the knowledge you have accumulated during your life. The Adult is also ready to add any new information you choose to go out and get, such as the information in this book. It is the grown-up, decisive, calculating, serious, Mr. Spock part of your brain. Your best life decisions will be made by the Adult, if the Parent and Child allow that to happen.

Awareness comes from the Adult. When you see things through your conscious mind, you have the opportunity to evaluate your behaviors, beliefs and habits. Then you can consider viable, realistic, beneficial changes without the burden of the subconscious clutter messing up the Parent or Child portions of your personality.

Uncorrupted awareness of what you do, why you do it, and whether it is relevant and optimal for your life today is the starting point for all meaningful change. As you can see, it is also the most misunderstood and misinterpreted of the three steps.

Support

Once you have a handle on what habits you want and need to change, it is very helpful to have the support of other people who are involved in the same self-evaluation. Why? Mainly, because the reasons that support old habits will be somewhat illogical and possibly embarrassing – not the topic you are going to want to discuss with your regular "moan mob" during lunch. As soon as you are serious about identifying and attacking weak, ineffective habits, you are going to find that you will be more comfortable with other people who are challenging themselves in the same way. Conversely, you may begin to see the topics of the old "carp crowd" as pretty shallow and unimportant. This is the successful theory behind all support groups, such as Alcoholics Anonymous.

The Vocational Shrink Communications Training Program was developed to provide one way for members of a group to support each other in the workplace. It offers the ability for an entire department to address its habits from an equal footing and work towards a common goal. The key is to make the journey fun, rewarding and worth the ride. Equal support makes this possible, whereas going it alone has proven to be ineffective in establishing major, permanent change in the workplace or in life. Old habits are comfy, and when an attempt at change starts to jeopardize that comfort, it's surprisingly easy to justify the old habit and slide right back into a warm, cozy, negative pattern again.

Using a common tool, management is also able to interact in the process, both as an overseer of employee progress and as another source of change that can keep the process up to speed. Rarely are workplace issues confined to the employees only. Management's own habits, outdated procedures, and lack of human relations expertise are often key factors in holding a company back.

Most of today's current management books encourage a culture where supervisors take on a more supportive role, allowing employees to exercise their personal creativity and to take responsibility for their work. The more that employees feel empowered to control their work life, the more of their natural creativity and discretionary effort (that extra performance they bring to the workplace that the company gets for free) comes pouring out.

The Vocational Shrink's Communications Training Program is one of many tools that managers can use to help employees take more responsibility for themselves, their workplace attitudes, their personal productivity, and to evaluate the way they interact with each other. The more you as a manager do to simply provide the tools and let the employees use them as they see fit, the more long term benefit you will realize.

Practice

Habits are formed by practice. That is how the old ones were formed and any new habits will require the same repetitive practice to take root. Experts agree that if you consciously change the way you do something, and keep doing it differently for about 21 days, it will become a habit. Try this. Every morning (you may not know this yet, but it's true) you put your shoes on in the same order – right then left or left then right. Determine which way you do it habitually, and then consciously change it to the other way. Place a little note in your closet or on the mirror to remind you when you are getting dressed. If you stay with it, in about 21 days you will begin to put your shoes on this new way without thinking about it. While that is a simplistic example, it is exactly how all skills become habits. Writer and philosopher Henry David Thoreau said, "Things do not change; we do."

Everything from improving your memory to learning a foreign language to changing workplace habits will only change through repetitive attempts to stay on a new, initially uncomfortable track. This is the reason that a support group and a well-defined track are so important. Remember that life habits took your whole life to become engrained. Give them some time to become redirected or you will quickly lose heart and give up.

> *"Things do not change; we do."*
>
> — Henry David Thoreau

Practicing new skills as a team with a common goal is considered to be the most effective way to achieve significant and long-lasting changes. As a manager, you are the conductor of your workplace orchestra. You're responsible for the content, the tempo, and ultimately the symphony that will come forth. *The Vocational Shrink's Communications Training Program* can help focus your department's practice, keep it in perspective and, most importantly, make it fun and unthreatening to the employees. After all, it is their tenacity, persistence, and desire to change that will make progress a reality.

Chapter Three

A Ray of Sunshine in the Storm

Just when you were beginning to get a little overwhelmed and starting to wonder how all this can work for you and your company, here is that extra support I told you about earlier.

Because this is a business book meant to educate and inspire a diverse workforce, I am simply suggesting you consider the benefits of accessing a greater consciousness in a general way. Spirituality is a very personal experience and my view of it might work against the effectiveness of the message of this book if it could potentially be offensive to any of my readership.

I do, however, have a more complete version of my personal spiritual journey and how it impacted my life and success in the workplace and as an entrepreneur, trainer, and consultant. If you would care to read it and get a more thorough understanding of my personal views and opinions, email me and I'll be happy to send you a copy. Thanks!

Summation

My reason for developing *The Vocational Shrink Communications Training Program* and the *Ten Levels of Workplace Disillusionment* was to give employees a tool to use for identifying aspects of their personality and habit patterns that lead them to react to the stresses of the workplace in unhealthy ways. Once that is done, they are free to either accept this as their lot in life, or begin to go through a process of systematically changing some of their habits and take steps to become less likely to fall back into the negative spiral that the *Ten Levels* represent.

The ultimate choice we all have to consider is whether to become more effective in our current job, find a more fulfilling one, or quit the corporate life and venture out on our own. "In spite of all the warnings, nothing happens until the status quo becomes more painful than change," says writer Laurence Johnson Peter. An awareness of the reality of the status quo, and the belief that a change is both possible and advantageous, will come as you address and overcome your old, instinctive habits.

As managers begin making the *Ten Levels* material available in a nurturing way to their employees, the benefits of growth and individual improvements in performance and job satisfaction will be seeded and nurtured within the company and can directly impact the bottom line. This is certainly not guaranteed, as we mentioned before, because new insights by one's workers will bring new levels of confidence to them . . . and awareness of other possibilities for personal fulfillment. Be prepared to deal with this likelihood – the perfectly normal tendency for employees to "look around" or seek a change of scenery – , by proactively creating "cool" motivational opportunities and recognition programs *within* your firm that reward and incentify your employees for challenging themselves to develop new, more productive habit patterns.

As more people in your organization begin to implement these improved work habits, they'll be more likely to feel fulfilled and happy staying with you. This is the ultimate "win-win-win" situation. Each employee wins, their manager wins, and the whole organization wins. Fostering personal growth is one of the easiest and most rewarding ways to enjoy quantum gains in productivity for any organization, not to mention making everyone's job far less stressful and a lot more fun.

Now that you have some understanding of how employees react to workplace stress and how costly low morale and poor productivity can be, **Part II** and **Part III** of this book will address why frustration is so prevalent in today's organizations and how to fix it.

"If your people

think you truly care—

they look for ways

to bring their "A" Game

to work and

enjoy doing it."

Part 2

Why are They Doing It?

What the Experts Say About Emotional Engagement and The Secret to Turning Recognition Expenses into Profits

I began my career in a large corporate workplace, and then worked for a couple years in a small family business. This is where I met (and experienced) the people with the characteristics that have become known as *The Ten Levels of Workplace Disillusionment*. From that point on, I began a journey of discovery to determine why so many people were frustrated and unhappy at work, why they fell into negative habit patterns to survive and what this phenomenon was actually costing them and their employers.

After about seven years of research and observation, I found that there is one consistent similarity that transcends all companies and all workforces, no matter the industry, size, age group or location – it all comes down to perception. What employees perceive as their manager's motives behind what they do totally defines the value and effectiveness of the message. In other words, if your people think you truly care they look for ways to bring their "A" Game to work and enjoy doing it. If they perceive that you are just trying to get them to work harder by cracking the whip, they will disengage and do just enough to get by.

Amazingly, it's really that simple. And it happens consistently, due in large part to managers' lack of training and understanding of one simple fact – employees work for money, but they excel when they feel valued. Most managers are overworked, understaffed and barely get through their own daily workload, so based on the misguided belief that money is the key to performance, many will randomly toss dollars, gift cards, and poorly organized pats on the back at their people hoping it will motivate them to meet the company's goals. Deep down, most are thinking ... "gee, I wish they'd all just shut up and get back to work so we all can keep our jobs!"

In some ways the recognition industry itself is to blame, because many award vendors sell products, rather than help their client's use proper strategies to achieve higher levels of employee engagement and productivity. Manufacturers buy drill bits, but what they're really needing are holes. In the long run, the company who understands all of the intricacies of hole drilling, will be more successful than the ones who simply compete to provide the lowest bulk price on bits. Their clients will get a better cost per hole and higher quality holes by using the right tools in the proper way, while their competitors will burn up a lot of cheap bits, scrap more parts and wonder why they're losing ground.

In **Part II** I'll share what I've learned about the nature of employees and supervisors and how it works together to create the low productivity and workplace issues that leave so many people feeling like a rat in a maze. In **Part III**, we'll look at how easy it can be to turn this around and create a workplace that is happier, more fulfilling and best of all, WAY more profitable and fun to be in!

Chapter 4
What Went Wrong With Traditional Recognition Programs

The Top Five Recognition Objections

As a student of employee morale and performance for most of my life, I've always been fascinated about what brings out the most in people and how much that tends to differ from what their supervisors think. Let's start out by looking at the five most common objections HR professionals hear regarding traditional forms of recognition. Since many of these have become entitlement programs, they may already be on the chopping block when revenues get tight.

1. Employees would rather have cash or time off.

They WANT cash and time off, but what they NEED is to be shown in a genuine way by management that they are truly appreciated. This is a Right Brain (emotional) activity. Cash and cash equivalents are Left Brain (logical), so they do not carry the recognition message. This type of recognition can be perceived as "buying me off," which often feels insulting and counter-productive to employees, because it involves consideration of "what am I worth." Compensation-based incentives are an important part of your Performance Improvement strategy, but will only work after your employees are emotionally engaged by management.

2. I want to recognize what they've done for me lately, not for ducking every five years.

Your Performance Improvement Strategy will incent employees to perform specific behaviors. However, research shows that far greater improvement in productivity, retention, attitude and profitability come from showing love and respect to employees *first*, then sharing with them how they can help the company be more profitable. If they believe you truly value them as human beings, employees will bring their "A" Game and all that comes with it, for free!

3. All of the programs look the same.

I can't argue with you there . . . a crystal bowl is a crystal bowl. What's needed is a way of taking the pressure off of the award to carry the entire message. The best programs use a single strategy based on the company's mission and values that includes all of your recognition, motivation and performance improvement tools. The secret ingredient is training. This will show your managers and supervisors how each program works differently in impacting your employees as well as leading them to embrace recognition on a personal, emotional and financial level. This honest look at *"What's in it for Me"* is the key to creating a strong, meaningful and ongoing recognition culture that will be seen over time by employees as legitimate. *"Gee, they really do care about me!"* Once the communications are in place, you can freely combine a broad range of programs for Years of Service, Performance and Acknowledgement to fully engage all of your employees and offer a awards that will be appreciated, not or their retail value, but for their intrinsic meaning.

4. We're all too busy to hand out recognition awards.

Most people already understand that having more engaged, happier, motivated employees saves both money and time. Until recently, there hasn't been a technology tool that can handle the Communications,

Training, Awards, and Reporting to make it easy to put your strategy into practice. You're actually already paying for it in lower productivity and higher recruiting and training costs due to voluntary turnover. Today's high tech, flexible platforms can help you wrap your arms around all of your performance initiatives, get management and participants engaged, and prove a significant Return on Investment, all with minimal time and effort by management. If you make it easy, structure it to be consistent and track it to prove its working, your recognition and performance strategy will pay big dividends.

5. Our employees don't have the loyalty they used to have and don't care about that old-fashioned stuff any more.

This is a common perception, but is based on survey questions that in many cases may yield the wrong impression. The very act of asking employees how they would prefer to be recognized carries with it a company's lack of understanding and interest. If employees perceive that you really don't care and are just going through the motions, they will ask for the money every time. If they were lying on the Psychiatrist's couch and asked why they work for you, however, it would have very little to do with money, benefits and work hours. Their comments would center on their career opportunities, how they are kept informed and how much they feel genuinely appreciated. This is the secret to getting the most out of your employees and revitalizing the loyalty that you think is gone.

Get More Productivity for Less Money . . . Your Employees will Love You for It

Chapter 5
The Five Biggest Mistakes Managers Make in Recognizing their Employees

They're costing you money,
but are easy to fix

> Jennifer was at the end of her rope. It was time for a new job, one that would let her use all of her talents, creativity and experience. The exit interview was uneventful, and then she was finally free! Her manager, Roberta, was baffled. How could Jen leave? She was on the fast track, with great potential, numerous promotion opportunities and was a key member of the team. What went wrong? Sound familiar?

A recent study confirms that this vast divergence between employee satisfaction and management appraisal is quite common, as well as confusing and expensive to organizations today. How could an employee be so unhappy while management is thinking everything is fine? There are five big mistakes that when addressed properly will reduce unnecessary turnover and immediately improve morale, productivity and profits. With some minor changes in management's communication style, your employees will want to bring their "A Game" to work every day.

Mistake #1 – Not Being Believable!

All executives claims to value their people; but are employees getting the message? Recognition programs, incentives, bonuses and at-a-boys are common in most companies, but are often seen as manipulative by the very employees they're meant to incent. Why? There's a fine line between the perception of true appreciation and feeling that you're just "throwing them a bone." Unfortunately, With staffing down, workloads up and everyone busier than ever, it's easy for a manager's recognition efforts to be perceived at just going through the motions, not coming from the heart. When your managers understand what's in it for them and begin to "Make it Real", their interactions are seen as genuine, with the employee in mind, not as leverage that benefits the company and leaves workers feeling like nothing more than a piece of meat.

Mistake #2 – Not Being Organized

Once your employees begin to believe you truly care about them, the next mistake relates to the number of disjointed programs companies use to recognize and reward their people. Each has its own history, function, author and responsible party, so there's no easy way to tell if they're working. It's impossible to properly train your management team how to use them correctly and in the right order, so effectiveness suffers.

By coordinating all of your employee communications, training, recognition and performance processes into one organized system, you can understand and control costs, manage and rate results and get the most for your investment in people.

Mistake #3 – Not Using a Strategy

An organized approach is great, but the system won't last is if it's not tied to a strategy based on the company's core values and goals. Strategic planning is a leadership function that allows all employees to understand where they fit into the total scheme of things and how their performance directly affects the organization.

After employees begin to see that they are all on the same team, marching in the same direction for the same reasons, synergy happens and your combined recognition efforts yield much more than the sum of the individual parts.

Mistake #4 – Not Having Management Buy-in

Even if you solve Mistakes #1 through #3 completely, your best efforts are likely to fail if you don't have strong, honest and consistent support from the top. Companies can use live kickoff events, and/or a professionally produced video featuring one or more top executives to not only launch any new program, but then continue to demonstrate their passion and dedication to the goals and objectives over time. Employees are very quick to see through any signs of the company being disingenuous.

Poor upper management involvement is one of the signs that you're using recognition as a manipulative lever, not an appreciation boost. To keep your top executives intrigued, committees must present program enhancements that show significant and measurable results, not just emotional blue sky and hype.

Mistake #5 – Not Following Through

Any program, no matter how exciting, rich, well organized or effectively supported, will lose its momentum over time if it's not fully integrated into your company's performance management culture. This is by far the most overlooked weakness in many recognition strategies and it's very disappointing after you've done so much right. A quality reporting system along with an empowered team prepared to manage the information is critical to keeping your programs relevant, fresh, interesting and profitable. The true test of a well functioning recognition strategy is when you can quantitatively prove to your CFO that it's turning expenses into profits over time. We incorporate measurable processes such as referrals, productivity changes, turnover, recruiting costs, profitability work well.

The five mistakes are quite common, extremely costly, but relatively easy to avoid with some simple communications training and the ability to look at entitlement programs with an open mind. Yes, they are called entitlements, because that's what your awards programs become if they are left alone for very long. It's nobody's fault, so rather than point fingers, just decide to address each mistake in order from #1 to #5, gain support and then develop a measurable set of initiatives that will make the best use of your company's dollars. The good news is that today's tools and technology solutions make it easy to develop, measure and analyze an effective recognition strategy.

"Why is it that when the company

offered the very thing

that employees seemed to want,

that it fell short

of carrying the

important message?"

Chapter 6
Cash Just Isn't Enough!

How to get more from, without paying more to, employees
—and they'll love you for it!

When surveyed, employees consistently ask for cash, but research shows that it's the least effective form of recognition. How come?

> Steve is a loyal employee who enjoys his work, is productive and reliable – the model employee. He was surprised when his 10 year service award package offered him cash as an option. It wasn't like he couldn't use a few extra bucks, but the fact that his employer was able to put a price tag on ten years of his life left him feeling a little cold and confused.

Why is it that when the company offered the very thing that employees seemed to want, that it fell short of carrying the important message – "We care about you and are glad you're on our team?" Maybe it has something to do with the question. Asking employees what they want implies that you don't know and really don't care all that much. The moment that employees think that you are using recognition more out of obligation than desire, they will emotionally disengage, feel a bit insulted, and give you the answer they think you want to hear – "Aw, what the heck, just give me a gift card!"

This actually has a lot more to do with perception than logic. Employees want so much to be genuinely appreciated, that the minute you give them the smallest hint that you're attempting to manipulate them with carrots and sticks, you lose.

It's really just about doing a few very basic things right and in the correct order. This requires training supervisors to understand some straightforward principles, realize that it's to their personal benefit to make recognition a powerful management tool (appeal to their natural self interests – in a good way) and communicate more effectively so their people believe they mean it.

Once honest emotional engagement is achieved, you'll be amazed at how quickly financial incentives can take you and your firm to another level of measurable, bankable ROI that will have everybody wanting more. It's an educational challenge that too many companies ignore, but are paying for over and over again.

Here are three ideas to consider:

1. No one disagrees that cash is important. However, you owe it to yourself and to your stockholders to do what's best with the company's money. Program tracking data overwhelmingly supports the fact that well-designed incentives out-perform cash by more than 2 to 1, as well as carry far lower tax consequences. Supervisors will embrace these tools when they understand their value, see what's in it for them, and have a clear, well-defined path to run on. You can give a gift valued at 1% of an employee's salary, and if done enthusiastically, they'll feel the love. But, give them a 1% bonus or raise and they're looking at the classifieds. Same dollars, totally different result–it's all about perception!

2. Most companies use a variety of disjointed programs to recognize and reward their people. Even if the programs are working, it's impossible to determine the level of participation and financial return. Imagine if you orchestrated all of the tools used to communicate with employees, so they could be properly measured, kept relevant to company goals and you could easily teach your supervisors the proper way to implement them. This is called an Umbrella Recognition

Strategy and the benefits are numerous.

3. As you begin to evaluate your current recognition programs, you'll be surprised at both the amount of money leaking out of the organization in various ways and why employees may be confused. Our team recommends a Four Cornerstones approach:

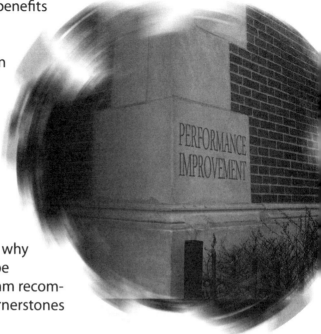

- **Communications** – People need to see where they fit in the overall scheme of things. Every employee wants to know the direction of the organization and the plan to get there. Communication addresses the "what to do" and provides a professional, well organized theme.

- **Training** – Managers need to know how to give recognition rather than just presenting awards. Training focuses on the "how to do" and is an important element to Performance Improvement.

- **Reinforcement** – Recognition is not an event, it's a process. Employees need to "want to," but how do we achieve this emotional engagement? It's done by validating. Employees must feel important and appreciated when they go the extra mile.

- **Measurements** – Things that are measured tend to improve. Measurements address the "how are we doing."

"With the vision and strategy in place, the objectives and responsibilities of each employee to support the strategy must be determined. This is the most overlooked part of performance improvement programs, because it requires responsibility and can often be uncomfortable. Outstanding employees want to be measured and ineffective employees want to remain invisible.

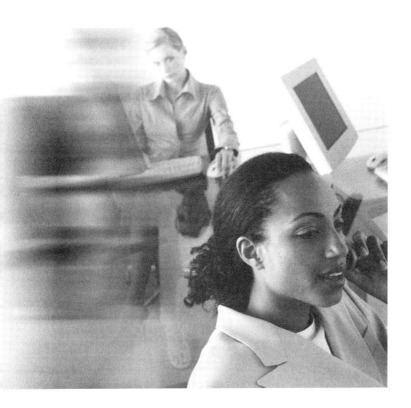

Chapter 7
How to Turn HR Expenses into Profits

Nobody's got new money to spend, but there are some simple ways to get more returns for fewer dollars and be able to prove it to your CFO!

The only good thing about today's challenging economy is that many established recognition and performance programs are open for review that might not hit the radar in healthier economic times. Everyone is looking for ways to make sure they're getting the most benefit from the dollars they're currently spending to recognize and award their people; or better yet . . . how to get even *better results for less money!*

> Joe works as an Engineer in a large manufacturing plant. Every month, he and his colleges anxiously await the company newsletter to view the photo of the General Manager and see if he was wearing a tie. When the weather heats up, in late May or early June, the newsletter displays an open collar photo, so this is the signal for everyone to take off their ties for the summer.

While this is a fun exercise and an appreciated casual Arizona dress code, Joe wonders, "Who the heck is this guy? Wouldn't it be great if he just wandered by every now and then and acknowledged us?" What Joe is experiencing is the very basics of good employee recognition; something termed Management by Walking Around (or in this case, the lack thereof).

In order to stay in touch with the people who report directly to you, simply walk around, talk to them, share with them, observe them, and don't be critical. If you do this with all your employees on a regular basis, you will quickly identify where they are succeeding, where they are struggling, and where they need help.

As a natural by-product of this technique, a trust relationship builds up between employees and their managers. The employees will feel like their managers know what they're doing and the managers will have a better rapport to address issues, both good and bad, with their employees. Here are five keys that will help:

1. **Visit everyone**
   This means getting out of your office and being visible. If you haven't done this in the past, initially it may be a bit awkward for you and your staff. But over time, they'll begin to see this as your management style and you'll be seen more as a "player coach" and less as "the boss." Make sure you don't have any agenda in mind. Just be available, present and interested. Your people will enjoy knowing that you're there, you're engaged and you practice what you preach. You'll also get a better feel for the way your organization runs and be a part of developing a relaxed, trusting and productive team environment.

2. **Stay positive**
   This one is easy; just keep a smile on your face and a twinkle in your eyes. Once your employees realize that you're wandering around because you like being there, not as a way of checking up on them, you'll find that you'll be more comfortably involved in your organization's day-to-day activity. Not that you need to know every detail of the

work going on in every department, just be accessible, upbeat and present in the operations of your business. Be careful not to undermine the management style or activities of your supervisors; it's still their team and their responsibility. Just be a part of the team and use this time to support your appreciation and respect for your people.

3. **Be genuine**
   Today's employees are discerning and quickly pick up on any insincerity they perceive in management. Be friendly, interested, open and vulnerable – I call this "Making it Real" and it's all about treating people the way you'd like to be treated. Be careful here, because if you're too involved, it can appear that you have a hidden agenda. That impression undermines trust and people will clam up around you. Instead, be yourself and let conversations flow in an easy way. Here again, don't get into too many specifics, particularly about their work or their responsibilities (that's their supervisor's job).

4. **Make sure it's not all business**
   Initially, you should make your interactions with employees almost totally NOT about business. Your first objective is to engage them emotionally and make sure that you're seen as a team member, not a boss. As they begin to trust you more, they will open up more about business issues. If you find that specific business issues come up, include the supervisor, so you don't make this a platform for people to go over their bosses head; this will backfire on you.

5. **Don't expect results right away**
   Depending on how involved you have been in the past, it will take time for your efforts to be accepted. Don't rush it and don't appear frustrated if you don't initially get honest and open communication. This approach is foreign to many employees and they will be looking for your hidden agenda. That's fine, but will fade as they begin to realize that it's for real.

Since 1993, when IBM had their first layoffs in history, there has been a growing acceptance of the misnomer that loyalty is dead.

So what does this have to do with turning expenses into profits? First, it's an extremely effective way of engaging employees emotionally. It's also easy and free! The theory is supported by a vast amount of research from experts such as the Gallup Organization all the way back to Abraham Maslow, who agree that appealing to employees' self esteem (their desire to be Loved and Respected) is where real engagement begins. Relationships are the foundation on which effective recognition is built and good relationships are built on trust. If you don't have trust-based relationships with your people you will waste your money and time trying to buy their discretionary performance.

Here are three strategies our team finds helpful as you share this with your managers:

1 It's All About Perception

The secret to effective recognition is employee perception. If managers are seen as just going through the motions, employees won't buy it. They'll feel underappreciated, and will ask you to "show me the money".

Any time employees ask for money rather than recognition, it's a sign of a training problem, not an awards problem.

However, when supervisors see Recognition and Performance Improvement as valuable tools that can actually make their job easier, they'll get behind your program initiatives and "Make it Real!" You've got to win over your managers and supervisors before you can expect them to win over their subordinates.

2 Look Through Your Employees' Eyes

As supervisors become more aware of how they tend to view things differently than their subordinates you are on track to overcoming the reason for most of the frustration, reduced productivity, turnover, and lack of cooperation in your company.

A George Mason University study by Professor Kenneth Kovach, shows that while employees consistently rate recognition and being informed near the top and good pay around the middle on their list of things that motivate them at work, most supervisors assume that good pay is at the top and recognition and being informed (another way of saying Love and Respect) are near the bottom on these employee surveys.

Until your employees believe you truly value them as human beings, any efforts you use to motivate them will be seem as manipulation and will turn them off. Management's understanding of what motivates employees is often flawed, and the moment your intentions are viewed as company-focused rather than from the heart, you begin to lose them emotionally. Make sure that any actions you use to improve performance follow engagement practices that make people feel valued as members of your team, not just a cog in a big machine.

3 Do it in the Right Order

Most companies already have a variety of training, recognition and incentive programs in place, but they are probably not being used in the correct order. It's a lot like dealing with kids; if they don't know you love them, your well-meaning discipline can come across as mean-spirited, self-serving and more about your convenience than their betterment. Our team suggests leading with Recognition (Love and Respect), then offering Performance Improvement opportunities (Share the Wealth) and finally special awards for high achievement (Specific Acknowledgement).

When you step back and view all of the ways you communicate with your employees as one cohesive strategy, rather than a group of unrelated awards programs, you will quickly be able to identify overlap, redundancy and areas of confusion. Then, as you relaunch using a training-based approach that puts your people's emotional needs first, you will enjoy both up-front savings and measurable ROI that will surprise and please you and your management team.

> If you like the information in Chapters 5, 6 and 7 and want to share it with your team, you can download them as separate .pdf articles from my website at www.SchaeferRecognitionGroup.com. Click the Media tab, then the Articles button.

Get More Productivity for Less Money . . . Your Employees will Love You for It

Part 3

How Can You Fix It?

Introducing the Umbrella Recognition Solution to Help you Save Money, Improve Results and Prove it to the CFO!

Current technology makes it possible to easily track performance against measureable objectives and drill down by company, division, location, department, manager and employee.

Chapter 8

The Umbrella Recognition Solution

Most clients use a disjointed array of programs to recognize and reward their employees. Even if they're working, it's difficult to evaluate participation, effectiveness and cost. What if you could orchestrate all of your Award/Reward initiatives, to optimize employee performance with a Comprehensive Recognition Strategy?

This idea is not new. Take retail for example. Our society has been morphing from a number of small, independently owned specialty shops to large big-box stores for years. Costco, Wal-Mart and Target rule the retail sector and have run off all but the most unique, upscale boutiques and creative stores. Remember the small office supply stores we used to go to for paper clips, desk accessories, and desk top equipment? Staples and Office Depot have put an end to those.

So too the small book store has fallen prey to Borders and Barnes & Noble, not to mention Internet players like Amazon. Most of the remaining private bookstores specialize in antiques and first editions. The movie *You've Got Mail* does a great job of depicting the emotional cost of this trend and how even a groundswell of media support won't stop our addiction to bulk discount stores.

People want to have their cake and eat it too. We wax eloquently about the virtues of the small, specialty shop – the service, impassioned proprietor, and quaint well-stocked shelves, but then we go to Costco and Wal-Mart for the cheaper price. You can't have it both ways, and in the end, low cost rules.

While cost is the primary driver in retail consolidation, it gets a bit more complicated with corporate purchasing. Getting the best price is certainly a factor, but with downsizing and a struggling economy, my corporate clients are also concerned with convenience, efficiency and the ability to outsource more of the support functions. Let's look at how the Umbrella Strategy works in each of these areas.

Minimizing Program Costs

There's one foolproof way to take your recognition program costs to the bare minimum – cancel the program all together! Silly, you say, but you'd be surprised at how many companies I consult with are considering this option, because they don't have a viable way of proving to upper management that they are making a good investment. Frankly, a lot of programs have become nothing more than entitlements, so this may not be totally unwarranted, but let's take the long term view.

An Umbrella Strategy begins with an evaluation of all of your current recognition programs and incentive initiatives. This allows you to drop or modify the programs with overlapping objectives, enhance the ones that stand to offer measurable results and organize them in the most effective implementation order. These three actions will assure that you are spending only what is necessary to get the results you desire.

Supervisor and Employee Training

One of the problems with multiple programs is the inability to educate supervisors and employees on how to use them all correctly and in the proper sequence. We suggest three types of training to remedy this:

1 Train employees and supervisors on your new program, so they understand the options to participate, what they can earn, and how each initiative impacts the company. If people aren't clear on the components of the program and it isn't front-of-mind, you won't get good involvement. Nothing's more wasteful than spending time and money to set up a new program, only to have disappointing participation numbers.

2 While knowing what to do is important, understanding what's in it for them and choosing to become enthusiastically involved is even more essential. Use management training to demonstrate how small changes in communication style show that you truly care about your employees, as opposed to creating the impression that you're just trying to manipulate their behavior by dangling carrots. This sounds simple, but it is often overlooked. Assuming that your harried managers will get excited and support the new program just because you're pumped up is a mistake.

3 I created *The Vocational Shrink Communications Training Program* to make communications training easy and fun. These tools will help employees and their supervisors become aware of negative habit patterns, so they can modify behaviors that cause frustration, lead to wasted time and cost you a lot of money. It's good to make this a cooperative effort and convince managers that if they let down their guard a little, be vulnerable and participative, most employees will meet them half way. By making this a game, you are engaging people's right brain – the creative, emotional side, which is where honest behavior change begins. People make changes emotionally, then justify it logically.

Chapter Eight

Reinforcement/Rewards

While they won't come right out and say it, everybody wants to know, "What's in it for me?" They won't ask, because it sounds selfish and deep down they want to help make their workplace better, but it's a natural question that you might as well address up front. Even if you haven't studied the research, most of us instinctively realize that money isn't as meaningful to people as tangible awards that they can earn. It's kind of like when you celebrated a birthday when you were a kid and grandma put a $10 bill in your card. While the money is nice, even a ten-year-old knows that she did it on the way to the party in the car – not a lot of forethought and not too personal.

A 2004 University of Chicago study found a simple way to prove it, and found out something else interesting in the process. They set up two teams to compete in a game designed to measure improvements in performance. One team was incentified with tangible rewards, while the other team was offered the same reward value in cash. At the end of the game the team competing for rewards improved by 39% and the group going for cash improved performance by 15%. That significant difference said it all, but then they put in a twist. As they were handing out the cash, they casually turned to the rewards group and ask how many of them would prefer cash instead. 78% jumped on it!

Wow, that's confusing, but what does that teach us? Well, first it says " . . . don't ask such a dumb question", but it really tells us more. It reinforces my belief that the

The Umbrella Recognition Solution

very question is suspect. Asking employees what they want, or presuming that cash is the answer, subtly insults their intelligence and supports their belief in your ulterior motives – that you're only offering them incentives to manipulate their behavior for your benefit, not theirs.

The researchers asked an additional question that was also quite revealing. They asked the 78% group that switched to cash after actually performing better with the potential of winning a tangible award if they were going to use the cash to purchase the award they had won. Not surprisingly, the people most interested in the cash were also the ones least likely to use the money to buy that award. So what is the lesson here? First, don't make the mistake of using cash, even though it's what the majority ask for. Second, when offering incentive rewards make sure you provide high quality, unique awards that most people don't buy for themselves normally.

Employees like options, the more the better. Older workers tend to go for tangible items, such as golf clubs, grandfather clocks and luggage. Today's younger employees favor technology items like digital cameras, DVD players and travel packages. The best services offer thousands of creative, current rewards and exciting travel options that are available on line and updated regularly.

Chapter Eight •

Measurement/Analysis

The most overlooked part of many recognition programs is the evaluation and improvement process. Over time, programs tend to become accepted forms of compensation, leading to an entitlement culture that minimizes results. A good solution partner monitors, evaluates, reports and makes recommendations that help you keep your program fresh, relevant and in step with your goals and mission.

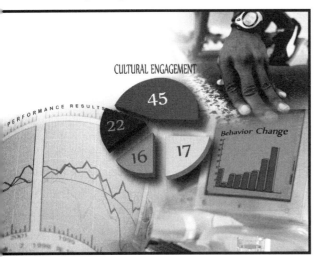

This area gets a lot of lip service and looks good in proposals, using lots of charts and graphs. In reality, it's where you need to be most vigilant and where a good partner is involved every step of the way. Technology allows you to custom tune your reporting to be simple, drillable and available to management, so your umbrella becomes a tool, not just a program.

Performance Management

This is the ultimate goal of your umbrella solution and where you will begin to see the ROI results that you need to keep the program growing as part of your company's culture. Don't let this sound overwhelming, as it's easier than you think. If you've set up the umbrella properly, there should be no surprises here; just trackable statistics that make it possible to hold everyone accountable for the results they've agreed are important.

Current technology makes it possible to easily track performance against measureable objectives and drill down by company, division, location, department, manager and employee. Once people see this system in place, they realize that there's no place to hide, so as long as the expectations are realistic and obtainable, and both your management team and employees buy in on a personal and emotional level, the results are both significant and lasting.

Get More Productivity for Less Money . . . Your Employees will Love You for It

Chapter 9
The Three Steps to Successful Recognition and Performance Improvement Structure and Implementation

After more than 25 years and having worked with hundreds of clients and the best partners in the industry, my team and I find that the most effective solutions use a three step approach to achieve employee optimization:

Step 1 – Evaluation and Recommendations

Since most companies already have a disjointed array of existing programs in place, as well as other measurable initiatives in mind that they haven't yet gotten around to developing into programs, we will first provide an assessment of your current recognition and incentive programs, as well as rate the morale and attitudes of your people. We'll use this information to develop a comprehensive Analysis and Recommendations report that gives us a good place to begin discussing how we can help your firm.

This exercise identifies all current costs, program acceptance, effectiveness of existing programs, and the potential benefits of integrating new ones. In many cases this alone leads to significant cost savings as we eliminate overlap, complexity and begin to see areas where well-meaning motivation and recognition tools have become entitlements.

Step 2 – Supervisor and Employee Training

Once we have developed an organized and accepted group of recommendations, we then introduce management training tools to help improve communications, engage employees, and set the stage for a more strategic approach to recognition. The types and amount of training depend on the size, structure and current levels of employee engagement, as well as your time frame in establishing more complete solutions.

This is the missing link that allows great ideas to become profitable actions. It's also where we help your management team see the personal benefits of embracing a structured approach to employee engagement. Only when all levels of management are on board, educated and enthusiastic can we you get the most out of the time and money you invest, so this step is probably the most important (and sadly, the most often overlooked) part of an Umbrella Solution.

Step 3 – Customized Recognition Solution

Finally, we'll propose an Umbrella Recognition Solution that orchestrates all of your recognition and incentive initiatives within a robust technology platform to minimize current costs, improve your results and use our customized reporting to prove it. Together our goal will be to turn current expenses into profits and share the good news with your CFO!

This may sound simplistic, but remember, the best solutions are often the easiest. Steps 1 and 2 set you up to get the most benefit from the least number of components. This makes your strategy easier use, easier to train and easier to get employees to participate in wholeheartedly. It all starts with a new communication style that stresses honest, genuine appreciation and care, then helps everyone start on the same page, and finally culminates in a clean, simple package of exciting recognition and performance improvement tools that are aligned and utilized in the proper order by an enthusiastic management team.

Visit www.SchaeferRecognitionGroup.com to learn more about how an Umbrella Recognition Solution can work for you.

Get More Productivity for Less Money . . . Your Employees will Love You for It

Chapter 10
A Combination of New and Traditional Tools

The best solutions involve a combination of old and new solutions and vary depending on the type of organization, the culture and the nature of the employee base. In this chapter I'll highlight all of the various program components that we find useful in helping clients optimize their time and budgets.

1. If it Ain't Broke Don't Fix it

This is probably the most common scenario we encounter when we meet and interview clients. A new HR team has inherited a weak, ineffective older program and while they may not know the solution to the problem, they are astutely aware that what they are spending their time and money on now is not working anywhere near as well as it could. It's lasted this long, because it's never been the top thing on the to-do list and it seems to be working okay.

The most common problem seems to be in the service award arena, where a program has grown to include a large array of lifestyle (retail) award choices, many easily shopped on eBay and other online close-out sites. This not only dilutes the perceived value of awards, but leaves employees more aware of the dollar value of their length of service than the appreciation their award represents.

This trend began in the late 90's as a response to growing employee dissatisfaction with the more traditional, logoed merchandise that made up the majority of the award selections in their programs. We now know that when employees complain about the award selection, it's more a sign of poor presentations than awards. The easy solution was to add more stuff and make it things that they can use on a daily basis.

This quick fix worked for a while, but with the growth of the Internet and the expansion of search engine technology, what it has also done is put a big flashing light on recognition budgets that do not motivate people. The primary message of "it's the thought that counts" has been replaced with "here's what your time is worth," and it's beginning to generate frustration and dissatisfaction among the very people it's supposed to entice.

2. The Secret is in Creativity and Uniqueness, Not More Stuff

There are several alternatives that make it easy to enhance a stale program while making your employees feel valued, not bought off.

Option 1 –

This is the easiest solution to implement and involves simply moving the lifestyle (retail) awards over to a points-based platform where they are earned for performance improvement initiatives, not length of service. The service awards continue to be presented as a series of budgeted plateau selections, but contain only long lasting, logoed, memento items that carry the enduring message of employee value and are not easily converted to cash value with a 30-second Internet search.

The added advantage of setting up the points platform is that you are now able to add and continuously modify your performance incentives, so employees get engaged in a growing variety of opportunities to participate in improving the company's bottom line while sharing in the rewards. The key to this approach is in training your managers to make sure that the service award experience truly shows that you value your employees as human beings and appreciate them being on your team. Then, they will automatically embrace opportunities to help the team and make the company grow.

Option 2 –

For clients who feel that their employees are best engaged by having the opportunity to grow their points bank in a large variety of ways, we can implement a program where the their length of service is recognized by a small, inexpensive logoed item in a customized gift presentation box, along with a quantity of points equal to your desired service budget. This approach helps pump up the points levels, so they can qualify for higher quality items in the online catalog without diminishing their feelings of symbolic value. It does this without divulging the cash value of their service contributions, so they respond more favorably and are continuously reminded of their value to the company.

The other huge advantage of Option 2 is that it eliminates the need for paper selection catalogs (if appropriate within your technology capabilities). No more back orders, shipping issues, discontinued items or Internet shopping for closeouts. Electronics in particular are subject to regular updates, so this eliminates the chance of employees finding the award pictured in the brochure is the "old model."

Option 3 –

A growing trend is to go custom and many of our clients are finding this to be a great way to both simplify their program logistics and make their offerings more personalized to the organization. One way to do this is with a Single Item Program, where we develop a series of totally custom awards, one for each service milestone. You can see an example of this at **http://www.SchaeferRecognitionGroup.com/phoenix-suns-award.html**. This program for the US Airways Arena employees features a group of custom crystal awards that replicate symbols unique to their people and carry tremendous trophy value.

An even more impressive custom solution is our Journey Award. This approach uses a custom-designed sculpture that is built throughout a career with your firm. A good example can be seen at: **http://www.SchaeferRecognitionGroup.com/product-demo-sub.html**. This is Matson Navigation's service award sculpture based on a crystal container ship that get's loaded with solid crystal containers as each employee meets five year milestones.

The key to going custom is in combining programs within a single strategy that is well communicated and supported by energized managers who demonstrate a team spirit and excitement for employee longevity and contributions. Using a training-based kick off and well written instructions, we can help make length of service part of an appreciated and well-defined career path that ties seamlessly with performance opportunities that make sense, have personal value and tie into the organization's goals and mission.

Summary and Conclusions

Since I graduated from college, I have been fascinated with employee engagement, productivity and the growing costs of poor morale. Having experienced the realities of the corporate workplace from both sides of the fence, it has become increasingly clear to me that the solutions are both straight forward and easy to apply, if you look at them from a training-based focus and do them as part of a single strategy tied to your company's mission and goals.

We hope this book was been an easy and intriguing look at the What, Why and How of today's recognition and incentive challenges and has gotten you energized to look at ways to improve your company's workplace and culture. Let us know how it goes for you and we'll be happy to share your stories with others. Together, we can make the American workplace a more pleasant, profitable, productive place to spend the majority of our lives as we all strive to be all we can be.

For more information visit us at: **www.SchaeferRecognitionGroup.com.** We also invite you to follow us on Twitter, Facebook and LinkedIn to stay up–to-date on exciting developments in recognition, incentives and manager training.

Get More Productivity for Less Money . . . Your Employees will Love You for It

About the Author

I began my working life as a paper boy at age 13. I got a busboy job at 16 and worked for eight years in the restaurant business as a waiter in several Scottsdale, Arizona restaurants to pay my way through school.

Upon graduating from Arizona State University in 1980 with an Industrial Engineering degree, I worked for two years in a large manufacturing company.

Then, I spent two years with a small family owned manufacturing business before starting my own recognition award, incentive and gift business, Recognition Concepts, Inc.

While I can't speak for everyone just entering the workforce, for me, fresh out of college, employment was a real eye-opener. I was prepared from a knowledge basis, and knew how to gather and process information. What took me by surprise, though, as I began my career in a turbine engine manufacturing facility, was the vast range of competency I saw among people who were supposedly at the same job levels, and the time-wasting survival habits of people who had been there longer than I.

What I had expected to be a group of inspired, like-minded professionals turned out to be a stress-filled pecking order with a disproportionate amount of time being spent covering up weaknesses, or perceived weaknesses, in every department. I had just completed college, graduating with an Industrial Engineering degree, and found myself working alongside people with the same title and job description as mine, but who had previously worked as a drill press operator. It was a shock, and immediately put a lot of strain on these new relationships. I was the new guy with the fancy degree and that made these other guys nervous. It wasn't my fault, but there was always an underlying need for the old timers to show me what they could do and, by inference, what I couldn't.

On the shop floor, I got a quick lesson on how the machine operators could manipulate the process engineers into believing a certain machining operation took far longer than it really did. They thought managers were there to make them work harder, even though our job was actually to determine the true cost of making engine components. I got smart pretty quick, and figured out a way of talking to an operator about his job while I was actually timing the guy on the next machine. That way,

I could see what was really going into each operation.

I saw people jealously hoard work space and office furniture that were not necessary to their job function. I saw numbers manipulated to make programs look more complete, or performances more successful, than they really were. None of these actions individually would constitute criminal fraud, insubordination, or necessarily lead to catastrophic engine failures, yet it amazed me how much time and energy was wasted covering up inefficiencies rather than addressing them. Actively cooperating with whomever or whatever was required to improve quality (especially when the solutions seemed pretty obvious to me) sure appeared to be a superior option. I came to realize that our universities do a great job of imparting book knowledge, but a poor one of preparing us to get along with other people, work as teams, and overcome the inherent politics that come with competitive work situations.

After more than 20 years of working with major corporations to improve their employee recognition, motivation and incentive programs, I've seen a lot when it comes to what makes employees tick. With knowledge and understanding, employees and employers can work together to optimize the employment experience.

Most of all, I believe that all people have the capacity to become far more than they think they can be, and that the resources required are freely available, if they simply choose to make use of them. *The Ten Levels of Workplace Disillusionment* may be a humorous take on things, but I hope it helps you take a serious look at the problem of low employee morale that still plagues so many companies in our country today.

There's much more to be said and discussed, because morale is an ongoing issue, and I hope I'll have the chance to meet with you face-to-face at a future training seminar. By now you can tell how much I enjoy working with clients to offer management training, recognition and incentive programs in and to help organizations like yours maximize their most important asset - people!

About the Illustrator

Brian Freeman attended Phoenix Institute of Technology where he studied Architectural Illustration.

He soon realized that his aptitude for drawing and painting people exceeded his knowledge of architecture.

He found work as a mural painter and illustrator in Tempe, Arizona where he eventually met John Schaefer. That meeting turned into a lasting friendship with John, who has utilized Brian's design and illustration talents on a number of corporate montage projects for the PaintMyStory® division of Recognition Concepts, Inc.

By the way, what started as a doodled caricature of John on the margin of a preliminary layout turned into the basis of many *"Ten Levels"* illustrations found in this book. "I have always loved the little caricature that Brian did of me," says John. "I framed it and it has hung over my desk for the past ten years, reminding me, in a humorous way, to never give up or take myself too seriously. When I realized that some fun illustrations would be perfect to personalize this book, the choice was immediate and obvious. Brian's cartoons always make me laugh!"

Brian works as a fine artist in several mediums, and teaches drawing and painting with pastels. He lives with his wife Pam in Tucson, Arizona with their four children, two dogs and cat.

Get More Productivity for Less Money . . . Your Employees will Love You for It

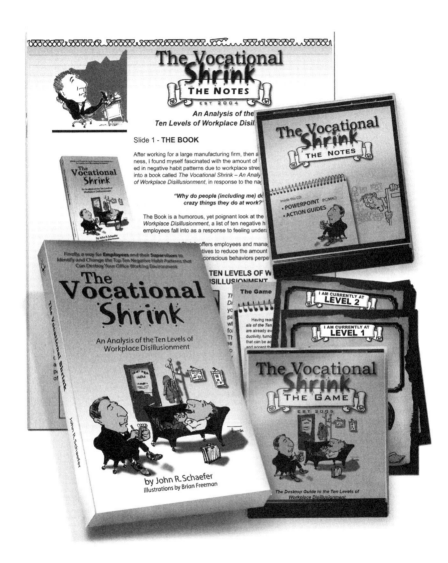

The Vocational Shrink Communications Training Program - Game and Action Guide

The purpose of the *Vocational Shrink Communications Training Program* is to help make people aware of the negative habit patterns they utilize in their workplace, counterproductive habits that allow them to slip back into various deep-seated and inefficient states. Our game depicting *Ten Levels of Workplace Disillusionment* seems to work best with groups of people who are equally willing to step back and look at themselves from a distance, be open-minded, and realize that true success in life starts when a person takes charge of his or her own actions. Used as part of a training regimen in a workplace setting can lead to shared fun, effortless education, and hopefully growing morale among all who participate. Management support and acknowledgement of the values this exercise represents will allow your company to make the best use of program and other materials at a departmental level or companywide.

> *Level 2's will fight it, Level 4's will misunderstand it, Level 6's will make fun of it, Level 9's will be scared of it but overall, most people will find our communications game to be a fun and ultimately valuable tool that helps put a finger on the core of many of their personal issues, as well as a number of the organization's problems. If it yields a happy, more productive workforce, management will love it.*

Having worked in a number of jobs prior to starting my own business, I can honestly say that it sure would have been nice to have it as a proactive morale training resource back then. From all accounts, though, life in the workforce hasn't changed all that much in the past 25 years. Remember that the awareness generated by the *Ten Levels* of Workplace Disillusionment is for personal growth of the participants, not to be used judgmentally or negatively. The security created by a group of understanding friends (even the Level 6's can be serious from time to time) is paramount in supporting a person as they modify their behavior. Greater confidence and improved self-esteem will begin to permeate the workplace as employees become aware of, and deal with, negative habits, idiosyncrasies, and subconscious reaction patterns. Abraham Maslow, the famous psychologist, said it this way, "If you plan on being anything less than you are capable of being, you will probably be unhappy all the days of your life."

If you experience particularly meaningful transformations or improvements in your organization, please let me know by emailing me at **john@SchaeferRecognitionGroup.com**. I would like to share your success and feedback with other customers, which will enhance their experience with the program.

Now, let the Games begin!

To order additional copies of

Get More Productivity for Less Money . . . Your Employees will Love You for It!

by **John Schaefer** - *America's Employee Recognition Expert*

visit:
- www.SchaeferRecognitionGroup.com
- call 1(888)646-6670, fax us at (623)572-1333
- or just mail a photocopy of the following page **Order Form** and clearly filled it in, include your check or credit card information to us at:

**Schaefer Recognition Group
7131 W. Planada Lane, Glendale, AZ 85310**

Order Form

☐ *Get More Productivity for Less Money ... Your Employees will Love You for It!*
           ___ x $19.95 = _____

☐ *The Vocational Shrink Communications Training Program – Book, Game and Action Guide*
           ___ x $99.95 = _____

Shipping & Handling: _____
($2.00 per book, $5.00 per Training Program)
Contact us for quantity shipping quote.

Tax : _____
(AZ residents add 9.3%)

Total Enclosed: _____

☐ *Sign me up for The Employee Recognition Expert Newsletter.*
☐ *Let me know about bulk pricing on Books and Training Programs.*
☐ *Contact me about The Umbrella Recognition Solution that will save me money, improve my results and let me prove it to my CFO.*

Name: _____

Company: _____

Title: _____

Address: _____

City, State, Zip: _____

Phone: _____

Email: _____

Credit Card Number: [_____]

Expiration Date _____/_____ 3 Digit Authorization Code: _____

John Schaefer
America's Employee Recognition Expert

Schaefer Recognition Group
7131 W. Planada Lane • Glendale, AZ 85310
(888) 646-6670
www.SchaeferRecognitionGroup.com
john@SchaeferRecognitionGroup.com

Get More Productivity for Less Money... Your Employees will Love You for It

John Schaefer
America's Employee Recognition Expert

John Schaefer helps organizations succeed by optimizing their most valuable asset – people. When engaged supervisors convince your employees that they truly care, and genuinely mean it, your firm begins to see significant results. The goal, he tells managers, is to *"Make it Real!"*

This Industrial Engineer with a degree from Arizona State University worked for a 6000 employee manufacturer, then a small family business. Schaefer's expectation was to be a valued component of an inspired, like-minded group of professionals, however his early career turned out to be a lesson in the stress-filled pecking order with a disproportionate amount of time being spent covering up weaknesses, manipulating information and pointing fingers. *Sound familiar?*

He set out to do something about the frustration and anxiety that he witnessed in the workplace which often led to unique survival habits among his co-workers. Those personal experiences along with wit and a passion for helping people is what Schaefer brings with him every time he talks to clients about getting the most out of the employment experience. In 1989 he formed his own recognition awards company then a few years later, after finding his old notes, he created **The Ten Levels of Workplace Disillusionment** and **The Vocational Shrink Game and Action Guide.** Though written as a humorous view of workplace craziness, it actually takes a serious look at the problems of low employee morale and high turnover which still plague so many companies today. Many of the causes and some of the solutions for these destructive job-inspired behaviors are presented in his book and accompanying game.

After more than 25 years of working with major corporations, Schaefer knows what makes employees tick. His manager training program *"Why Should Supervisors Care? Getting to the bottom of what they're really thinking—"What's in it For Me?"* shows how subtle changes in the way they communicate can help managers and their employees greatly improve their work life. "I'm convinced that everyone has the capacity to become far more effective and fulfilled than they think they can be," shares Schaefer. All of the resources required are freely available, if they simply choose to use them enthusiastically and in the right sequence.

Today John Schaefer and his team at Schaefer Recognition Group help companies realize and react to what he calls the Employer/Employee Disconnect. He's sought out for his straight talk, loved for his humor and dedicated to helping people have more fun, be more productive and save their companies tons of money.

Warren Struhl

Since leaving the corporate world as vice president of JMB Realty, one of the largest commercial real estate firms in the U.S., Warren has focused on entrepreneurial endeavors, repeatedly identifying well-established industries and product categories ready for change and building successful businesses around them.

He founded his first business, PaperDirect in 1988 at the age of 25. After building it to $100 million in sales, the business was sold to a Fortune 500 company in 1993. He built upon the PaperDirect success, launching, investing in and advising a portfolio of companies including Successories, Register.com, Genesis Direct, White Cloud Consumer Products, American Registry and Poster.com

In 2003, Warren founded Dale & Thomas Popcorn. By reinventing the stale, ready-to-eat popcorn category, its major brand Popcorn, Indiana quickly became the first national, premium kettle-cooked popcorn brand. Today, Dale & Thomas and Popcorn, Indiana products are sold in over 150,000 locations nationwide.

Warren's entrepreneurial successes have been featured on CNBC, Fox and MSNBC, among others. He has written several articles for Inc. magazine advising entrepreneurs on what they need to know to launch a new company.

In 1994, Warren was the Ernst and Young Entrepreneur of the Year in New Jersey as was named Entrepreneur of the Week by Yahoo Finance in 2008.

Warren's first book, *Starting Them Up – An Inside Look at the Life of a Start-Up* will be published late in 2010.